STUDIES IN THE UK ECONOMY

Deindustrialization

Stephen Bazen
University of Bordeaux

and

Tony Thirlwall
University of Kent at Canterbury

Second edition

Series Editor
Bryan Hurl

HEINEMANN
EDUCATIONAL

Heinemann Educational Books Ltd.
Halley Court, Jordan Hill, Oxford OX2 8EJ

OXFORD   LONDON   EDINBURGH
MELBOURNE   MADRID   ATHENS
BOLOGNA   PARIS   SYDNEY
AUCKLAND   SINGAPORE   TOKYO
IBADAN   NAIROBI   HARARE
GABORONE   PORTSMOUTH NH (USA)

First published 1989

Second Edition 1992

British Library Cataloguing in Publication Data

A catalogue record for this book is available from the British Library

ISBN 0 435 33022 5

Typeset and illustrated by Taurus Graphics, Abingdon, Oxon.

Printed and bound in Great Britain by Athenaeum Press Ltd

94 95 96 97 5 4 3 2

Acknowledgements

The authors are grateful to Bryan Hurl for his editing of the final version of the book and to Celine Noronha for typing the original manuscript.

The Publishers would like to thank the following for permission to reproduce copyright material:

The Age for the article and cartoon on pp. 85–89; Associated Examining Board for the questions on pp. 50, 51, 63, 64, and 84; Central Statistical Office for the tables on pp. 9, 12, 17, 19, 31, 36, 39, 40, 42–43, 57, and 62; *Economic Affairs* for the article on pp. 23–24 by Stephen Bazen and Tony Thirwall; the *Financial Times* for the letter on p. 58 by Tony Thirlwall, the article on p. 60 by Samuel Brittan and the article on p. 77; the *Independent on Sunday* for the article on pp. 79–80 by Bill Martin; Joint Matriculation Board for the questions on pp. 30, 49, and 64; Macmillan for the tables on p. 28; the *Observer* for the article on p. 61 by Tony Thirwall; the OECD for the tables on pp. 5, 64 and 65; Oxford & Cambridge Schools Examination Board for the questions on pp. 8, 16, 17, 30, 31, 49 and 84; Richard Willson for the cartoon on p. 81; Southern Universities Joint Board for the questions on pp. 8, 30 and 49; the *Sunday Times* for the graph on p. 65; the *Times Newspapers Ltd* for the *Times* editorial on p. 22, the letter on p. 23 from the Chairman of the House of Lords, the article on pp. 47–48 by David Blake and the article on p. 74; University of Cambridge Local Examinations Syndicate for the questions on pp. 8, 16, 30, 31, 49 and 84; University of London Examinations and Assessment Council (formerly UL School Examinations Board) for the questions on pp. 8, 73 and 74; University of Oxford Delegacy of Local Examinations for the question on p. 64.

The Publishers have made every effort to contact the correct copyright holders. However, if any material has been incorrectly acknowledged, the Publishers will be pleased to make the necessary arrangements at the earliest opportunity.

Contents

Preface to Second Edition

The revelation in 1983 that, for the first time since the Industrial Revolution, the United Kingdom's balance of payments in manufactured goods plunged into deficit served to spotlight the underlying structural deterioration in the economy which the gains from North Sea oil have failed to mask. Indeed, the contribution of manufacturing to the GDP (gross domestic product) is now only 20 per cent; three decades ago it was 33 per cent.

As the 1980s progressed, so the supply side reforms produced claims of a 'Thatcher miracle'. As Professor Thirlwall asked of my own pupils, 'If what has been happening to manufacturing industry and the balance of trade in manufactures is an economic miracle, what then is an economic disaster?' Now that we are into the 1990s, post Thatcher, and with a clear mandate for John Major, Tony Thirlwall is still – persistently – questioning along these lines.

The importance of deindustrialization is being reflected in examination questions. It is a classic example of the dynamic nature of economics that the choice of Deindustrialization as a Special Topic Study at A/S level by two exam boards, justifies the country's two foremost experts on it providing an up-to-date, authoritative account for this level of study.

Bryan Hurl
Series Editor

Introduction

Alice thought 'It's sure to make some change in my size; and, as it can't possibly make me larger, it must make me smaller, I suppose.' Lewis Carroll

The subject matter of the phenomenon of deindustrialization is a very important one, and a very topical one in the United Kingdom economy. It affects all our lives, as did the decline in the relative and absolute importance of agriculture in the British economy two centuries ago, and as the shrinkage of the agricultural sector in today's poorer countries in Asia, Africa and Latin America affects the lives of people there. If employment or output in industry declines, this has implications for the overall level of employment and unemployment, for the rate of growth of output (i.e. gross domestic product or GDP), and for the economy's balance of payments position if exports and imports are dominated by industrial goods. All this has further implications for a country's exchange rate (and, therefore, also the rate of inflation), for its rate of interest, and for the whole of economic policy. To study deindustrialization therefore involves a consideration of both micro- and macroeconomic issues.

In the United Kingdom there is a special interest in the phenomenon of deindustrialization because, in comparison with other countries, the process seems to have been the most severe, particularly in terms of the loss of jobs in manufacturing industry and the fall in the share of industrial output in total output. There is an amusing acronymic classification of the countries of the world into HICs (hardly industrialized countries), PICs (partly industrialized countries), NICs (newly industrialized countries), MICs (mature industrialized countries), and DICs (decadent industrialized countries). The United Kingdom is a prime DIC! As our economy apparently moves (without intervention) from being an industrial society to a **post-industrial** society, there are some very important questions to ask concerning the future of work: whether an economy can sustain itself simply by specialization in service-type activities, and, if not, what is the role of government, and what policies might it pursue, to arrest the decline of industry. This book attempts to address some of the important issues involved.

1

What is deindustrialization?

'Deindustrialization has gatecrashed the literature, thereby avoiding the entrance fee of a definition.'   F. Blackaby

In 1966, employment in the UK manufacturing sector reached a peak of 9.1 million. Between 1966 and 1990 it fell by 4 million. In the same period, employment in the service sector increased by 3.4 million while total employment (excluding the self-employed) was stagnant. The stagnation of employment was also associated with a very slow growth of manufacturing output. From 1966 to the oil supply crisis of 1973, manufacturing output increased by 25 per cent, or at an annual growth rate of 3.5 per cent. From 1973 to 1979 (when Mrs Thatcher came to power) manufacturing output fell by 4.1 per cent. Between 1979 and 1982, during the deepest recession since the early 1930s, manufacturing output fell by a further 14 per cent, and only in 1987 did it again reach its 1979 level.

Since then, it increased during the mini-boom of 1986–89, but then fell back to its 1987 (or 1979) level. Overall, manufacturing output has increased by only 19 per cent in the 25 years since 1966 – a rate of growth of less than 1 per cent a year.

The definition should be cause-free and possess universality
The term deindustrialization refers to a long-term contraction of the manufacturing sector (although some commentators also include mining and quarrying, construction, and gas, electricity and water), but how it should be measured is a source of disagreement. What is needed is an operational definition which gauges the seriousness of the decline of the manufacturing sector. It should also be a **cause-free definition** in the sense that it should not prejudge the cause(s). Some definitions of deindustrialization do prejudge the cause(s), rather as the definition of inflation as 'too much money chasing too few goods' prejudges the cause of inflation, and therefore precludes wider analysis.

A further desirable property for an operational definition is that it possesses **universality**. It should be neither time- nor place-specific. *It should be easily observable and permit international comparisons.*

On this basis we can distinguish between the various definitions that have been suggested. We shall briefly consider two of them.

Singh's definition of deindustrialization

Dr Singh of Cambridge University suggests that deindustrialization occurs when 'the manufacturing sector, without losing price or cost competitiveness, is unable to export enough to pay for the full-employment level of imports'. In other words, deindustrialization *results* from the failure of the manufacturing sector to generate enough foreign exchange in order for the economy to be run at a level of activity corresponding to the full employment of labour.

This is illustrated in Figure 1, which measures imports and exports on the vertical axis and national income on the horizontal axis. Imports are assumed to rise with income, while exports are assumed to be determined by incomes abroad and not by incomes at home. At full employment, planned imports exceed exports, and equilibrium on the balance of payments requires a lower level of income Y_1 which is not sufficient to generate full employment. Jobs in manufacturing (and other activities) are lost.

It is clear, however, that this definition is not cause-free, since deindustrialization is defined in terms of the trade performance of the manufacturing sector. While, in fact, this may be the most convincing *explanation* of deindustrialization (see later), the cause is still prejudged and therefore Singh's definition is not satisfactory.

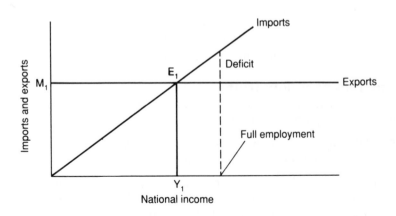

Figure 1 An illustration of Singh's analysis of deindustrialization

Furthermore, his definition does not possess universality. Most of the non-oil-producing developing countries find it difficult to export enough to pay for all the imports they require for the development process, yet their manufacturing sectors are generally expanding, and therefore these countries are not deindustrializing.

While Singh's view of the causes of deindustrialization in the UK are convincing, his definition of the process is unsatisfactory.

Bacon and Eltis's definition of deindustrialization

Another popular definition was once given by two economists from Oxford University, Bacon and Eltis. They claimed that the excessive growth of resources employed in the non-market sector of the UK economy (consisting mainly of government activities whose outputs are either not marketed or are sold at a loss) had reduced the resources available for the market sector (especially manufacturing), which had consequently contracted. A larger non-market sector had starved the market sector of labour and investment resources which it required to grow.

Deindustrialization is thus defined in terms of the growth of the non-market sector, but again the cause is prejudged. It is possible, in the competition for resources in a fully employed economy, for the growth of one sector to bid resources away from another. On the other hand, in conditions where resources are unemployed or growing, it is quite possible for the non-market sector to be growing while the manufacturing sector is also expanding satisfactorily in terms of employment and output.

The Bacon-Eltis thesis was first put forward with reference to post-war Britain, and then extended to other countries. Subsequent research, however, showed that their explanation of the loss of manufacturing jobs in Britain could not be satisfactorily explained simply by the growth of employment in government service activities, see page 35.

The two best definitions

The two best definitions of deindustrialization which are cause-free and not time- and place-specific are

- a declining *share* of total employment in manufacturing, and
- an *absolute* decline in employment in manufacturing.

Table 1 (OECD data) shows that most developed economies have experienced a declining share of civilian employment in the manufacturing sector since 1960, and Table 2 (also OECD data) shows a falling share of output in manufacturing relative to GDP. However, this may not reflect an absolute contraction of the manufacturing sector. A falling *share* may simply be the result of employment in manufacturing growing at a slower rate than total employment, and in this sense deindustrialization may not be a cause for concern. A declining share of employment in manufacturing might be expected in the process of development as the composition of demand changes away from manufactured goods towards service-type activities, including leisure pursuits and foreign travel.

On the other hand, an *absolute* decline in manufacturing employment *is* a cause for concern, and this will also mean a declining share of manufacturing employment if employment in other sectors is growing faster, or contracting at a slower rate than employment in manufacturing.

Table 1 The share of manufacturing in total civilian employment in certain OECD countries

	1960	*1970*	*1979*	*1989*
UK	**36.0**	**34.5**	**29.3**	**20.8**
Canada	23.7	22.3	19.9	17.0
USA	27.1	26.4	22.7	18.5
Japan	21.5	27.0	24.3	24.2
France	27.5	27.8	26.1	21.3
Germany	37.0	39.4	34.3	31.6
Italy	23.0	27.8	26.7	22.7
Netherlands	30.6	26.4	22.3	19.0
Norway	25.3	26.7	20.5	15.8

Table 2 The share of manufacturing in total output in OECD countries

	1960	*1970*	*1979*	*1989*
UK	**32.1**	**28.1**	**24.9**	**19.3**
Canada	23.3	20.4	19.1	16.5
USA	28.6	25.7	23.8	22.5*
Japan	33.9	35.9	30.1	30.2
France	29.1	28.7	27.0	20.8
Germany	40.3	38.2	34.1	29.9
Italy	28.5	28.9	30.6	28.1
Netherlands	33.6	28.2	19.0	20.2
Norway	21.3	21.8	18.2	12.5

* 1987 figure.

In fact, the only situation in which an absolute decline in employment in manufacturing might provide a misleading picture of the health of the economy is if technology is expanding very rapidly so that labour productivity is also expanding very rapidly, leading to falls in employment. However, as we argue below, technical progress should not be the enemy of employment in the long run since technical progress creates new products, new wants and new manufacturing industries – at least it has done so historically. Technical progress and productivity growth are also vital for countries to remain competitive in the world economy, without which the demand for exports will fall and make employment worse. This consideration give rise to a distinction in the literature between positive and negative deindustrialization.

Positive and negative deindustrialization

Employment in manufacturing declines when the rate of growth of output is lower than the rate of growth of labour productivity. (Since labour productivity is measured as output per person, it follows that the rate of growth of employment equals the rate of growth of output minus the rate of growth of productivity.) If employment is falling because a high rate of growth of output is being outstripped by an even higher rate of growth of productivity, then it is difficult to regard this decline as a cause for concern. Indeed, it may be thought desirable that the number of hours worked per week, weeks worked per year, and the length of working life should fall secularly as the economy moves into the post-industrial stage. This is **positive deindustrialization**. However, if it is a low growth of output that is being exceeded by a mediocre rate of growth of productivity, then the decline of employment is attributable to a sluggish growth of output and the wealth to finance increased leisure time is not being created. The country is likely to be getting relatively poorer compared with other countries. This is **negative deindustrialization**.

Thus, *positive* deindustrialization occurs when the share of employment in manufacturing falls because of rapid productivity growth, but where displaced labour is absorbed into the non-manufacturing sector. The economy remains at full employment and the GDP per capita is higher. This can be seen by the movement from A to B in Figure 2. On the other hand, *negative* deindustrialization results from a decline in the share of manufacturing in total employment, owing to a slow growth or decline in demand for manufacturing output, and where the labour displaced results in unemployment rather than being absorbed into the non-manufacturing sector. Here the fall in manufacturing

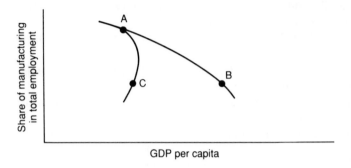

Figure 2 Positive and negative deindustrialization

employment is associated with stagnation and unemployment. This would be represented by the movement from A to C in Figure 2.

Deindustrialization can therefore be associated with benefits if it is accompanied by fast output growth, or cause severe problems if it is associated with stagnant output. When we come to examine the performance of the manufacturing sector in the UK, we shall see that *the deindustrialization experienced has been predominantly of the negative kind*.

The definition of deindustrialization we prefer in this book is:

a long-term absolute decline of employment in the manufacturing sector.

This definition is cause-free and permits historical and international comparisons. It also makes clear the significance of deindustrialization for unemployment. If the labour force, defined as all those wishing to work at a particular time, does not decrease in size, a reduction in employment in manufacturing will lead to unemployment unless jobs are created at a fast enough rate elsewhere in the economy – in particular in the service sector.

KEY WORDS

Cause-free definition	Bacon and Eltis's definition
Universality	Positive deindustrialization
Singh's definition	Negative deindustrialization

Reading list

Bacon, R. and Eltis, W., *Britain's Economic Problem: Too Few Producers*, 2nd edn, Macmillan, 1978.

Harrison, B. *et al.*, Chapter 32 in *Introductory Economics*, Macmillan, 1992.

Healey, N. and Levačić, R., Chapter 2 in *Supply Side Economics*, 2nd edn, Heinemann Educational, 1992.

Maunder *et al.*, *Economics Explained*, 2nd edn, Collins Educational, 1991, pp. 538–39.

National Institute of Economic and Social Research (NIESR), Chapter 6 in *The UK Economy*, 2nd edn, Heinemann Educational, 1993.

Singh, A., 'A Third World view', Chapter 4 of *Money Talks* (Horrox, H. and McCredie, G., eds), Thames Methuen, 1983.

Essay topics

1. Explain what you understand by deindustrialization. What are the potential benefits of deindustrialization to an economy? (Southern Universities Joint Board, 1989)
2. 'The effects of deindustrialization are varied but not necessarily always a matter for concern'. Elaborate and comment upon this point of view. (Combined boards of Oxford & Cambridge/ Southern Universities/Cambridge Local, AS-level, 1990)

Data Response Question 1

Industrial output

This task is based on a question set by the University of London School Examinations Board. Study Table A, which is abridged from *CSO Blue Book* 1991, and answer the following questions.

1. Define and explain the meaning of 'index' numbers of output at constant factor cost.
2. Describe the main trends in output in the different sectors of the economy during the period shown.
3. How might these trends be explained?
4. What additional information would you require in order to give a fuller assessment of British economic performance between 1980 and 1990?
5. Explain GDP average estimate.

Table A Gross domestic product at constant factor cost: by industry of output (1985 = 100)

	1980	1981	1982	1983	1984	1985	1986	1987	1988	1989	1990
Agriculture, forestry and fishing	83.0	85.2	92.3	87.3	104.7	100.0	97.1	97.9	97.4	101.2	104.4
Production											
Total energy and water supply	82.6	86.5	91.6	96.8	88.8	100.0	105.0	103.9	99.3	89.6	88.8
Total manufacturing	96.8	91.0	91.2	93.8	97.4	100.0	101.3	106.6	114.1	118.9	118.3
Total production	92.6	89.6	91.4	94.7	94.8	100.0	102.4	105.7	109.5	109.9	109.2
Construction	89.9	82.9	89.4	95.1	99.6	100.0	104.5	112.7	122.9	130.4	131.8
Service industries:											
Distribution, hotels and catering; repairs	87.3	86.0	87.6	91.5	96.2	100.0	104.6	111.4	117.9	121.8	122.6
Total transport and communication	89.7	89.9	89.0	91.6	96.1	100.0	104.3	112.5	118.5	125.3	128.0
Banking, finance, insurance, business services	73	76	81	87	94	100	111	122	133	139	144
Public administration, national defence and compulsory social security	102	102	100	100	100	100	100	100	99	99	101
Education and health services	95	96	97	99	99	100	101	104	107	108	108
Other services	87	86	86	89	95	100	105	113	118	121	123
Total services	88.9	89.2	90.5	93.4	97.0	100.0	103.9	109.4	114.0	117.4	119.4
Gross domestic product (output-based)	90.7	89.3	91.1	94.1	96.7	100.0	103.3	108.1	112.7	115.3	116.4
Gross domestic product (average estimate)	90.7	89.6	91.2	94.6	96.3	100.0	103.6	108.3	112.8	115.3	116.2

Chapter Two
The extent of deindustrialization

'*Unless the climate is changed so that steps can be taken to enlarge the manufacturing base, combat import penetration and stimulate the export of manufactured goods, as oil revenues diminish the country will experience adverse effects [which taken together] constitute a grave threat to the standard of living . . .*'. Report of House of Lords Select Committee on Overseas Trade

In this chapter we discuss deindustrialization as a long-term absolute decline in employment in the manufacturing sector in line with the definition given in the previous chapter.

Figure 3 shows the long-term decline of manufacturing employment in the UK, together with trends in employment in the service sector (including Public Administration), and in total employment for the period 1966–90. Since 1966, employment in manufacturing has followed a relentless downward trend. Between 1966 and 1979, just over 2.0 million jobs were lost in manufacturing, while a further 2.0 million were lost between 1979 and 1990. Employment in services grew rapidly between 1970 and 1980 – some 2.3 million jobs were created – after a period of relatively slow growth during the 1960s. Total employment (excluding the self-employed and the armed forces) fell after 1966 by 0.9 million up to 1972 and thereafter rose slightly, reaching a peak in 1979, and then fell dramatically in the recession of the early 1980s. Since then, employment has returned to its 1979 level.

The overall picture, therefore, is one of a long-term decline in manufacturing employment which reduced total employment in the late 1960s, but was counteracted by the growth of employment in services between 1972 and 1979. Between 1979 and 1983 manufacturing and total employment contracted together. Since 1983 manufacturing employment has continued to contract while total employment has grown.

In the late 1970s and early 1980s the UK economy experienced a severe **shock** (which we examine in detail in Chapter 5), the impact of which added a large cyclical component to the underlying structural decline. On our definition of deindustrialization, it has been a continuous process since 1966, which was vastly exacerbated by the events of

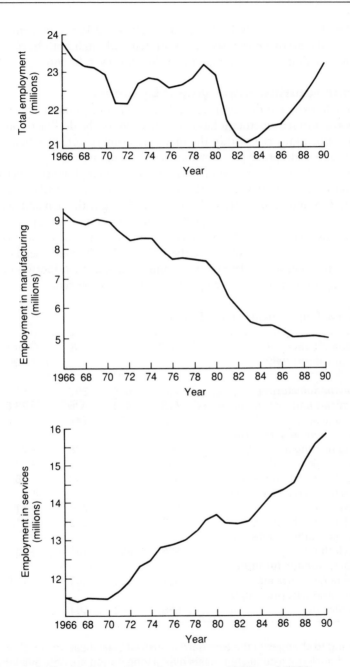

Figure 3 Employment trends between 1966 and 1990

the late 1970s and early 1980s. Between 1979 and 1982, total employment and employment in services both fell, although both have since recovered. Employment in manufacturing, however, has not.

Manufacturing employment by industry

Given the extent of the contraction of manufacturing employment, it is important to see whether it has been the result of the decline of one or two major industries within the manufacturing sector, or whether it has been a widespread phenomenon across all industries.

Table 3 shows changes in the absolute level of employment over the period 1972 to 1990, which is the longest run of figures available using the 1980 Standard Industrial Classification. Along with the manufacturing sector as a whole, in the majority of industries employment peaked in the 1960s and there has been a relentless decline since then in all major activities. Particularly badly hit in the 1970s and 1980s were metal manufacturing, motor vehicles and parts, and textiles, leather, footwear and clothing, all with declines in employment of over 50 per cent.

Table 3 Employment in manufacturing* (thousands)

Standard Industrial Classification (1980)	1972	1979	1990	Change 1972–90 (%)
Metal manufacturing	788	694	392	−50.3
Chemicals and man-made fibres	428	436	326	−23.8
Mechanical engineering	1057	1033	744	−29.6
Office machinery, electrical engineering and instruments	992	954	728	−26.6
Motor vehicles and parts	491	464	245	−50.1
Other transport equipment	403	376	248	−38.5
Metal goods not elsewhere specified	544	505	319	−41.4
Food, drink & tobacco	759	713	520	−31.5
Textiles, leather, footwear & clothing	986	800	491	−50.2
Timber, wooden furniture, rubber, plastics etc.	617	591	549	−11.0
Paper products, printing & publishing	558	542	484	−13.3

* Owing to changes in the Standard Industrial Classification, employment figures on a consistent basis over a long period are only available for Great Britain.

Source: Department of Employment *Gazette* (various issues)

Manufacturing employment by region

The maps in Figure 4 show the distribution of manufacturing employment across the eleven **standard regions** of the United Kingdom in 1966 and 1990. The mass of manufacturing industry and employment is concentrated down a central axis running from the North West, through the West Midlands into the South East of England. These three regions contain over 50 per cent of manufacturing employment. Between 1966 and 1979 when manufacturing employment fell by 2.0 million, or nearly 20 per cent, all regions suffered except the South West and East Anglia. The worst-hit regions were the North West and South East where manufacturing employment fell by 29.1 and 28.8 per cent, respectively.

The typically depressed regions

Between 1979 and 1990, manufacturing employment fell by a further 2.0 million, or nearly 30 per cent. Particularly badly hit during those 'Thatcher years' were Scotland, Northern Ireland, the North, North West – the typically depressed regions of the United Kingdom – but also the West Midlands and the South East. In all these regions, manufacturing employment declined by over one-third.

In terms of employment experience, the **north-south divide** has widened as a result of the economic policies (or lack of them) pursued since 1979. Manufacturing employment has also fallen in the 'south' as a whole but not to the same extent, and some of the decline has been offset by much higher employment growth in other sectors – particularly in services and construction – which has prevented unemployment from rising as fast as in the 'north'.

Regional disparities in employment growth and unemployment not only have welfare implications, but they can also affect adversely the functioning of the total economy. For example, demand pressure in the 'south' can affect wage inflation, the price of land and house prices, the effects of which 'spill over' into other regions causing a higher level of aggregate inflation for any given level of aggregate demand in the economy as a whole. Thus regional disparities can worsen the conflict between macroeconomic objectives. Only an active regional policy which discriminates in favour of depressed regions, as far as the location of economic activity is concerned, can cope with these problems of regional imbalance.

Britain compared with other industrialized countries

If employment in manufacturing in the rest of the industrialized world has declined over a long period, the process of deindustrialization in the

Figure 4 The regional dimension of deindustrialization 1966–90 (shows employment in manufacturing in thousands and the percentage decline)

UK might simply be considered as part of a decreasingly important role played by manufacturing activities in the world economy at large.

However, as Table 4 shows, of the 23 countries for which the comparison can be made, the majority of OECD countries experienced an *increase* in employment in their manufacturing sector between 1960 and 1989. No country experienced a decline in employment of the proportion experienced by the UK. Over the period 1960–89, employment fell by 39 per cent according to the OECD figures. If attention is confined to the shorter period 1960–79, the same conclusion holds.

Between 1979 and 1989 no OECD country experienced an absolute fall in manufacturing employment of the magnitude experienced by the UK. Although not alone in its experience, the UK is one of the few OECD countries to experience significant deindustrialization, and the reduction in manufacturing employment has been by far the most extensive in the UK since 1979.

Table 4 Manufacturing employment in OECD countries 1960–89* (thousands)

	1960	1979	Change 1960–79(%)	1989	Change 1960–89(%)
Canada	1 406†	2 047	+45.6	2 126	+51.2
USA	16 796	21 040	+25.3	21 652	+22.4
Japan	7 990	11 070	+38.5	14 840	+85.7
Australia	1 111	1 177	+5.9	1 236	+11.3
Austria	858	(850)	−1.0	910	+6.0
Belgium	1 043	888	−14.9	779	−25.3
Denmark‡	741	793	+7.0	715	−3.5
Finland	431	582	+35.0	525	+22.5
France	6 322	5 291	−16.3	4 585	−27.5
Germany	(9 433)§	(8 370)	−11.3	8 582	−9.0
Greece‡	598	994	+66.2	1 011	+69.1
Iceland‡	24	38	+58.3	42	+75.0
Ireland	168†	(228)	+35.7	215	+28.0
Italy¶	3 735	4 716	+26.3	4 729	+26.6
Luxembourg¶	53	58	+9.4	37	−30.2
Netherlands	1 082	(1037)	−4.2	1 152	+6.5
Norway	331	370	+11.8	308	−7.0
Portugal	571	(865)	+51.5	1 108	+94.1
Spain	2 009	2 742	+36.5	2 738	+36.3
Sweden‡	1 499	1 359	−9.3	1 315	−14.0
Switzerland‡	1 227	1 229	+0.1	1 234	0.0
Turkey	885	1 572	+77.6	2 216	+150.4
UK	**8 996**	**7 253**	**−19.3**	**5 512**	**−38.7**

Figures in brackets are not strictly comparable with previous years.
*Wage and salary earners in the manufacturing sector unless otherwise specified. †1961. ‡Civilian employment in industry. §1962. ¶Wage and salary earners in industry.

KEY WORDS

Shock   North-south divide
Standard regions

Reading list

Armstrong, H. and Taylor, J., *Regional Economics*, Heinemann Educational, 1990.

Paisley, R. and Quillfeldt, J., Exercises 13, 27 and 28 in *Economics Investigated*, Collins Educational, 1989.

Turner, P. and McCormick, B., 'The north–south divide', *Economic Review*, vol. 5, Sept. 1987.

Essay topics

1. Why are there regional variations in unemployment rates in the United Kingdom? To what extent would regional differences in pay reduce the divergences in unemployment rates? (University of Cambridge Local Examinations Syndicate, 1990)
2. Does the fact that the index of industrial production has been rising, and further growth is forecast, suggest that the problems of deindustrialization are over? (Oxford & Cambridge Schools Examination Board, 1988)
3. 'Current regional policy offers no solution to the growing problem of long-term unemployment'. Discuss. (Oxford & Cambridge Schools Examination Board, 1992)

Data Response Question 2

Deindustrialization

This task is based on a question set by the Oxford & Cambridge Schools Examination Board in 1990. Study Table A and answer the following questions.

1. Define 'deindustrialization'.
2. What symptoms of deindustrialization appear in Table A? Is there any evidence of its causes?
3. Are the trends a cause for concern?

Table A	1979	1986	1988
Index of manufacturing output (1980 = 100)	109.5	104.7	118.7
Share of manufacturing in total output (%)	27.3	23.0	23.9
Employment in manufacturing (thousands)	7259	5239	5152
Share of manufacturing in total employment (%)	31.3	24.3	22.7
Employment in services (thousands)	13 556	14 495	15 319
Share of services in total employment (%)	58.5	67.1	69.5
Balance of trade in manufactures (£ million)	+2 698	−8 055	−15 770
UK import penetration in manufactures (%)	26	33	38

Sources: *CSO National Income and Expenditure: Employment Gazette; British Business*

Chapter Three
Does deindustrialization matter?

If manufacturing industry contracts, there is a real danger that the whole economy will stagnate . . .

Having documented the decline of employment in the UK manufacturing sector by industry and by region, and seeing that it has generally been more pronounced than in other industrialized countries, it is now important that we consider the question of whether deindustrialization matters.

In this chapter we outline three important reasons why a strong manufacturing sector is both necessary and desirable for the overall health of the UK economy.

- Firstly, there are the obvious implications for unemployment.
- Secondly, it is widely recognized that the manufacturing sector has certain unique growth-inducing characteristics not found in other sectors of the economy.
- Thirdly, we emphasize the importance of manufacturing industry for a healthy balance of payments, and hence for the *growth* of the economy if it is not to be constrained by balance of payments deficits.

Historically, and up to as recently as 1982, Britain always had a surplus of trade in manufactured goods, which helped to pay for imports of food, raw materials and fuel; but now this is no longer true. If the economy is to grow faster and unemployment is to be substantially reduced, the performance of the UK manufacturing sector is of vital importance. If manufacturing industry contracts, there is a real danger that the whole economy will stagnate through a lack of technological dynamism and severe balance of payments constraints on growth.

Unemployment
Deindustrialization will lead to **unemployment** if the growth of employment elsewhere in the economy is insufficient to absorb the labour shed by the manufacturing sector (unless the size of the workforce declines).

Since 1966 deindustrialization has led to higher unemployment in the UK (see Table 5, the figures in which are taken from various issues of

Table 5 Changes in employment 1966–90 (thousands)

	1966–79*	1979–83†	1983–90
Change in labour force	+154	+241	+1826
Change in total employment‡	−959	−2106	+1788
Change in unemployment§	+1063	+1640	−1429
Change in employment in:			
Agriculture	−110	. −30	−51
Manufacturing	−2008	−1728	−479
Other production industries	−706	−268	−196
Services	+865	−81	+2328
Change in self-employment and armed forces	+90	+343	+1058

*Based on SIC 1968 classification. †Based on SIC 1980 classification. ‡Excluding the self-employed and armed forces. §Excluding school-leavers.

the *Annual Abstract of Statistics*). Agriculture and production industries other than manufacturing shed over 800 000 jobs between 1966 and 1979, while over two million jobs were lost in manufacturing itself. The increase in jobs created by the service sector was insufficient to absorb the loss of jobs in manufacturing – so that, together with the increase in the size of the labour force, unemployment rose by over one million. Then, between 1979 and 1983, employment fell in all of the sectors listed; manufacturing in particular lost 1.7 million jobs while unemployment rose by a similar number.

There has also been a large increase in self-employment. The contraction of the manufacturing sector still remains responsible for the high levels of unemployment.

Growth

A related, though conceptually distinct, worry about deindustrialization concerns the role that the manufacturing sector plays in the process of **economic growth**. It is often asserted that the manufacturing sector is the 'engine of growth', for reasons summed up in what have become known as **Kaldor's Growth Laws** (after Professor Nicholas Kaldor, the great Cambridge economist who died in 1986).

There are three laws to consider. The first law states that there is a strong positive relationship between the growth of manufacturing industry and the growth rate of the economy as a whole in a *causal* sense – and not simply because manufacturing activity constitutes a large fraction of the **gross domestic product** (GDP). The second and

19

third laws are concerned with accounting for this strong positive relationship.

The second law states that there is a strong positive relationship between the growth of manufacturing output and the rate of growth of productivity in manufacturing.

The third law states that there is a strong positive relationship between the rate at which manufacturing output and employment grows and the rate at which productivity grows outside manufacturing, because resources are used which would otherwise be unemployed or have a lower productivity.

The first growth law

Professor Kaldor, in his analysis of growth-rate differences between twelve OECD countries, found a strong correlation between the growth of manufacturing output and the growth of GDP; and the faster the growth of manufacturing *relative* to the growth of GDP, the faster the growth of national income. In other words, what distinguishes fast-growing countries from slow-growing countries is whether the *share* of manufacturing output in total output is increasing or not.

Since growth-rate differences between countries are largely accounted for by differences in productivity growth (that is, differences in the growth of output per person), rather than differences in the growth of the labour force, Kaldor concluded that there must be a relationship between the rate at which manufacturing output grows and the rate at which productivity grows inside and outside manufacturing. This was also confirmed by his research, and has been supported by other research. This leads to the second and third laws.

The second growth law

As far as productivity growth in manufacturing is concerned, Kaldor found that, on average, a 1 per cent growth of output leads to a 0.5 per cent increase in productivity growth. This relationship (the second law) arises from the existence of increasing returns to scale in the manufacturing sector, both static and dynamic.

Static increasing returns to scale means that if *all* inputs are increased, output rises by more than in proportion to the increase in inputs, leading to an increase in output per person. **Dynamic increasing returns** relate largely to technical progress embodied in capital goods, which means that the faster the rate of capital accumulation associated with output growth, the faster the rate of growth of labour productivity. An increase in the rate of growth of output therefore leads to a cumulative expansion via increased productivity.

These characteristics do not appear to be found in sectors other than manufacturing.

This second law is also sometimes known as *Verdoorn's Law*, after the Dutch economist P.J. Verdoorn who first mooted the relationship in 1949.

The third growth law

As far as productivity growth *outside* manufacturing is concerned, Kaldor found a strong negative relationship between productivity growth in the economy as a whole and employment growth outside manufacturing (holding employment growth in manufacturing constant), therefore indicating that fast employment growth in non-manufacturing activities slows up overall productivity growth, and vice versa. This is because, very often, there is only a very loose relationship between output and employment in sectors like agriculture, retailing and other service activities, so that when employment rises or falls, output hardly changes at all. This phenomenon is often referred to as **disguised unemployment.**

Disguised unemployment is very prevalent in the agricultural sector of Third World countries and in the petty service trades found in the urban areas; but it is a phenomenon also found in more industrialized economies.

Many activities outside manufacturing are also subject to **diminishing returns,** so that if the labour force is reduced, the marginal product of labour, and the overall level of productivity, rises.

The cumulative effect

Taken together, these three laws mean that a country which obtains an initial advantage in productive activities that have favourable growth characteristics will tend to sustain that advantage by exploiting increasing returns to scale, both static and dynamic, leading to higher productivity and competitiveness.

For example, a favourable shock which increases the rate of growth of output in manufacturing will lead to faster productivity growth, which in turn, by making goods more competitive, expands the demand for output, which again induces productivity growth, and so on. This is sometimes called a **virtuous circle of growth.** If, as we have observed in the UK since 1966, the rate of growth of manufacturing output has been stagnant or it declines, the opposite occurs, creating a **vicious circle** of low economic growth, low productivity growth, deteriorating competitiveness and the shedding of labour from the manufacturing sector owing to a lack of domestic and foreign demand for the products.

EDITORIAL IN *THE TIMES*, 7 MARCH 1991

MANUFACTURED CONCERN

Does manufacturing industry really matter? Yes, according to yesterday's report from the 12 nobles who make up the House of Lords committee on science and technology. Their lordships have been banging on about manufacturing for the best part of a decade, most notably in Lord Aldington's 1985 report on overseas trade. Gordon Brown, the Labour industry spokesman, is now able to praise the Lords committee in aid of the pro-manufacturing policies outlined by his party in its policy statement "Modern Manufacturing Strength", published last week. "Action is needed now to stop the decline of our manufacturing industry" say the peers. "The first objective . . . must be to modernise our manufacturing base", said Labour. The views of the Upper House and its historical political enemy coincide.

On further inspection, this concordance is less surprising than it may seem. These are peers of a very particular background. Of the committee's 12 members, ten, including the chairman, Lord Caldecote, have held senior jobs in or around manufacturing industry. One more, Lord Chapple, is a former leader of the electricians' union, which is strongly represented in manufacturing. Labour too has deep roots among those who make things, and their trade unions.

Vested interest, then, underlies both sets of proposals. They are supported, nevertheless, by an apparently impressive collection of facts. Employment in manufacturing has fallen from seven million to five million in a decade. The UK balance of trade in manufactures has deteriorated from a small surplus in 1979 to a deficit of £15 billion in 1989. British manufacturing is less profitable than that in France, America, Germany, Italy and Japan.

No one sensibly doubts the importance of "manufacturing"; it contributes a quarter of national output, and Britain cannot pay its way in the world selling services alone. But such figures are not all they seem. The divide between manufacturing and service industry is a statistician's artefact, revealing nearly nothing about the real world. Take for example a computer firm, marketing a mix of software and hardware. Is this a manufacturing company or a services company? How can you sell computers abroad if you do not sell software, and vice versa?

The evidence of decline is skimpy. True, employment in manufacturing has fallen. But this is a measure of its success in increasing productivity. True, since 1979 what is called manufacturing's share of national output has declined. But this is a product of the recession of the early 1980s, in which heavy industry bore the brunt. Between 1981 and 1989, according to the official figures, output in manufacturing and in services has grown at almost precisely the same rate.

The conditions that favour manufacturing industry are those that favour the economy as a whole: a growth-oriented macro-economic policy; a culture that encourages private enterprise; a state which remedies free market shortcomings in labour mobility and skills and in infrastructure. Proposals put forward by the Lords (and the Labour party) merit examination by a government that sometimes seems too timid in intervening to combat private sector inflexibilities. But they merit consideration as remedies for the enterprise economy as a whole.

A healthy economy supplies both goods and services. The Lords do their cause no good by a romantic attachment to the supposed economic virility of manufacturing as against supposedly effete services. The longstanding taunt that the non-manufacturing sector is "Mickey Mouse" and "candyfloss", usually from trade unionists worried that their factory power bases are being eroded, is simply out of date.

LETTER TO *THE TIMES*, 13 MARCH 1991

Critical balance of goods and services

From the Chairman of the House of Lords select committee on science and technology
Sir, I read with dismay the final paragraph of your leading article, "Manufactured concern" (March 7). This committee's concern about the plight of UK manufacturing industry is based on the evidence we received during the 12 months of our enquiry and not, as you suggest, on our "romantic attachment to the supposed economic virility of manufacturing as against supposedly effete services".

Balance of Trade
(£million, current prices)

Year	Services	Manufactures
1980	3653	5428
1981	3792	4497
1982	3022	2094
1983	4064	−2733
1984	4519	−4527
1985	6687	−3765
1986	6696	−6125
1987	6628	−8112
1988	4504	−15100
1989	4698	−16822
1990	n/a	−10883

The figures shown here, taken from the February *Monthly Review of External Trade Statistics*, support our concern.

Of course we recognise and welcome the substantial contribution of services to the UK economy. A healthy economy does indeed supply both goods and services. But UK industry's inability to produce the goods that the customer wants to buy has resulted in the current balance of trade deficit.

Service industry should not be seen as a substitute for manufacturing because many services are dependent on manufacturing and only 20 per cent of services are tradeable overseas. Moreover, at no time since 1986 has the balance of trade in services been sufficient to compensate for the deficit in manufactured goods.

Yours faithfully,
FLOWERS, Chairman,
Select committee on science and technology,
House of Lords.

Why Manufacturing Industry Matters

S. Bazen and A.P. Thirlwall

In the post-war years, Britain has experienced the most extreme form of deindustrialization of any country in the world.

It has suffered the severest decline in the share of manufacturing employment and output in total activity; the slowest growth of industrial output, and the largest contraction of employment in manufacturing industry.

Associated with these trends (and causally related, we believe) has been the slowest annual growth of GDP of any major industrialized country (averaging 2.7% from 1950 to 1972, and 1.9% from 1973 to 1986) and the slowest rate of growth of export volume. Most countries set themselves the macro-economic goals of full employment;

faster growth; balance of payments equilibrium (as an intermediate objective); and stable prices.

Deindustrialization on the scale experienced by Britain is not consistent with the achievement of these goals, and there is no evidence that service activities can adequately compensate. Let us take these goals in turn. **continued overleaf**

The current level of unemployment is appalling by any standards, and the unemployment record has worsened gradually through time. Employment in manufacturing peaked in 1966, and since then over four million jobs have been lost, two million prior to 1979, and over two million since the economic experiments of the Conservative government. In the 1970s, service employment rose to compensate, but since 1979 total employment has fallen by 1.35 million while unemployment has risen by 1.56 million. The expansion of service industries has not compensated for the decline in manufacturing. This is not surprising for two reasons. First, a part of the measured decline in manufacturing and the growth of service activity has been the result of a process of increased vertical integration within industry whereby tasks previously performed by manufacturing have been sub-contracted to specialist (service-type) agencies. This, in itself, means that services cannot be regarded as a *substitute* for manufacturing, but are part and parcel of the process of change in industrial organisation. Secondly, many services are dependent for their existence on manufacturing, and if the demand for manufactured output declines, so does the demand for services in a vicious spiral downwards.

Turning to the growth of GDP, there is a close association across countries between the growth of manufacturing and the pace of economic growth. The faster manufacturing output grows, the faster productivity growth in manufacturing tends to be. This is sometimes called Verdoorn's Law. This relation is associated with static and dynamic returns to scale, which characterises manufacturing. Such a relation is not nearly so marked in the case of service industries, and appears completely non-existent in land based activities. The second reason is that the faster manufacturing grows, the faster productivity growth outside manufacturing tends to be where there is disguised unemployment or low productivity.

This is still a major potential source of growth in some European countries which have a much larger agricultural sector than Britain.

As far as the balance of payments is concerned, the contraction of the British manufacturing industry is starting to have devastating consequences. Traditionally, Britain ran a deficit on visible trade financed by a surplus on the invisible account (i.e. earnings from insurance, shipping and other financial services provided by the City of London). Within the (negative) visible account, there was a surplus on manufactured trade which partially (but not entirely) helped to pay for a deficit in food and raw materials (including oil). In the last ten years or so, the situation has radically altered for the worse The surplus on trade in manufactures has gradually dwindled. In 1983, there was a deficit for the first time in British economic history, and now the deficit is a staggering £10 billion or more. At the same time, the surplus on oil is diminishing, and will shortly disappear. This leaves the traditional surplus on invisible account to pay not only for the deficit in trade in food and raw materials, but also for Britain's insatiable appetite for foreign manufactured goods. The situation is clearly not sustainable, since there is no evidence that the service sector can generate the export earnings to finance such huge deficits.

The present indifference to manufacturing seems destined to vindicate Napoleon's jibe about Britain being 'a nation of shopkeepers'. Services have an important part to play in the economy, but they do not provide the growth momentum of the manufacturing industry, nor can they be relied upon to substitute for the loss of employment and tradeable output caused by the weakness of manufacturing. The British economy is slipping into a gross state of imbalance with regard to the division of resources between manufacturing on the one hand and services on the other. A healthy economy requires a healthy manufacturing sector.

Source: *Economic Affairs*, April/May 1989

The balance of payments

While the foregoing laws can explain differences in the growth experience of countries, the initial impetus to the growth of manufacturing output is not determined. Historically, the stimulus has come from the agricultural sector in the early stages of development and from exports in the later stages.

One of the major reasons why Britain was the first country to industrialize was that it experienced an early agricultural revolution which raised productivity in agriculture and increased the demand for manufactured goods as inputs and as finished products. But Britain did not choose to specialize in agriculture, nor is it rich in raw materials. The lack of self-sufficiency in food and the paucity of raw materials leads us on to the third reason why deindustrialization matters, namely the **balance of payments**.

The UK needs to import foodstuffs and raw materials, and to pay for these (in order to maintain equilibrium on the balance of payments current account) the UK exports mainly manufactured goods, various services ('invisibles'), and more recently North Sea oil. North Sea oil production has already begun to level off and will generate lower export earnings in the future (unless the dollar price of oil rises by more than in proportion to the fall in output), which will increasingly leave exports of services and manufactured goods to pay for the necessary imports of food and raw materials (including oil in the future).

Traditionally, the balance of trade in goods (the **visible balance**) has been in deficit, although exports of manufactured goods used to exceed imports of manufactures. The latter is now no longer true. Since 1983 the balance of trade in manufactured goods has been in deficit, and the trend appears to be deteriorating. This means that only a surplus of trade in services (the **invisible balance**) is left to pay for food, raw material requirements and the appetite for foreign manufactured goods. This is not a sustainable situation, and without any improvement in the manufacturing trade balance, the growth of the whole economy will have to be slowed up to cut back imports.

This leads us to the important concept of **balance of payments constrained growth**, and the measurement of a country's balance of payments equilibrium growth rate.

Balance of payments equilibrium growth rate

Theory

For the current account of the balance of payments to balance, the value of exported goods and services must equal the value of imported goods and services. For an equilibrium to be preserved, the *rates of growth* of the values of exports and imports must be equal.

Elasticity

How fast the value of exports grows depends firstly on how fast export prices are growing; and secondly on how fast the demand for exports is growing which will depend partly on price competitiveness and partly on how fast world trade (or income) is growing.

The relationship between two growth rates is in economics called an **elasticity**; that is, an elasticity is the percentage change in one variable divided by the percentage change in another. Thus the relationship between the growth of exports and the growth rate of relative prices of home and foreign goods is called the *price elasticity of demand for exports*, and the relationship between the growth of exports and the growth of world income is called the *income elasticity of demand for exports*.

Likewise for imports. How fast the value of imports grows depends firstly on how fast import prices are growing; and secondly on how fast the demand for imports is growing, which will depend partly on how competitive imports are and partly on how fast income (or more accurately, expenditure) is growing within the country. The relationship between import growth and relative price changes is called the *price elasticity of demand for imports*, and the relationship between the growth of imports and the growth of domestic income is called the *income elasticity of demand for imports*.

If we make the assumption that in the long run there is very little change in the relative prices of exports and imports (measured in a common currency), then the growth of imports and exports is dominated by income changes at home and abroad. There will be a certain growth of domestic income which just keeps the growth of imports in line with the growth of exports. That growth of income consistent with balance of payments equilibrium on current account will equal the rate of growth of export volume divided by the income elasticity of demand for imports. This defines a country's *balance of payments constrained growth rate*, and is illustrated in Figure 5.

X_1 and X_2 show different levels of export *growth*. Lines OM_1 and OM_2 show the relationship between import growth and GDP growth, so that the slope of the curve measures the *income elasticity of demand for imports*. The steeper the curve the higher the income elasticity. Where X and M lines cross, this defines the GDP growth rate consistent with balance of payments equilibrium. It can be immediately seen that a country with a low export growth (X_1) and a high income elasticity of

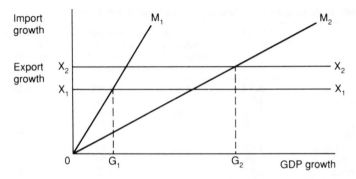

Figure 5 A country's balance of payments constrained growth rate

demand for imports (M_1) will have a lower growth rate (G_1) than a country with a higher growth of exports (X_2) and a lower income elasticity of demand for imports (M_2), whose growth rate will be G_2.

Empirical evidence
There is a lot of empirical evidence for the advanced industrialized countries that the actual experience of countries is very close to the growth rate predicted by the above model. That is, no country can grow for very long faster than the rate of growth consistent with balance of payments equilibrium on current account, because there is a limit to the ability and willingness to finance deficits.

Tables 6 and 7 give some evidence for a variety of countries over different time periods of fitting the foregoing analysis to data on export growth and the income elasticity of demand for imports, for comparison of the estimated growth with the actual growth experience. It will be noticed that the UK is estimated to have one of the lowest growth rates consistent with balance of payments equilibrium because its export record is so poor, and also has the worst growth record of any industrialized country. Japan, by contrast, has the highest balance of payments equilibrium growth rate, and has also experienced the fastest rate of growth, while at the same time running balance of payments surpluses because it has not been growing as fast as it could without going into balance of payments deficit.

From the point of view of economic policy in the UK, any programme that aims to increase economic growth, other than one based on trade, will soon run into a balance of payments constraint. If the UK economy is going to experience job-creating growth, either exports must grow more rapidly or measures must be implemented to reduce the income elasticity of demand for imports. We return to these issues in Chapter 6.

27

Table 6 Actual and equilibrium growth rates 1953–76

	Change in real GDP (%)	Change in export volume(%)	Income elasticity of demand for imports	Balance of payments equilibrium growth rate*
UK	**2.71**	**4.46**	**1.51**	**2.95**
France	4.95	8.78	1.62	5.42
Germany	4.96	9.99	1.89	5.29
Italy	4.96	12.09	2.25	5.37
Belgium	4.07	9.24	1.94	4.76
Netherlands	4.99	9.38	1.82	5.15
Denmark	3.58	6.77	1.31	5.17
Sweden	3.67	7.16	1.76	4.07
Canada	4.81	6.02	1.20	5.02
USA	3.23	5.88	1.51	3.89
Japan	8.55	16.18	1.23	13.15

*The second column divided by the third column.
Source: Thirlwall and Gibson (1992)

Table 7 Actual and equilibrium growth rates 1970–85

	Change in real GDP (%)	Change in export volume(%)	Income elasticity of demand for imports	Balance of payments equilibrium growth rate*
UK	**1.9**	**4.7**	**2.14**	**2.2**
France	3.5	6.3	2.42	2.6
Germany	2.4	5.0	1.92	2.6
Italy	2.6	5.2	2.83	1.8
Belgium	2.7	5.0	2.64	1.9
Netherlands	2.2	4.3	2.00	2.4
Norway	3.9	4.4	1.43	3.1
Sweden	2.2	3.8	2.53	1.5
Canada	3.4	5.0	1.70	2.8
USA	2.5	5.7	2.32	2.5

*The second column divided by the third column.
Source: Thirlwall and Gibson (1992)

Export of services

The model outlined above is based upon equilibrium on the current account of the balance of payments, so that a higher rate of growth of **exports of services** would serve as well as exports of manufactured goods. However, there are important reasons why the potential growth in exports of services may be limited in a way that the growth in exports of manufactured goods is not.

Firstly, as recently suggested by the House of Lords Committee on Overseas Trade (consult the reading list), trade in services is limited in the sense that only a small proportion of service output is tradeable (perhaps

20 per cent). A recent study by economists at the Bank of England pointed out that in 1979 the UK service sector exported only 11 per cent of its gross output (compared with 33 per cent in manufacturing).

Secondly, the sheer magnitude of manufactured exports is greater than that of service exports. In 1989, the value of finished and semi-finished manufactured exports was approximately £75 billion compared with service exports of only £30 billion.

Thirdly, in both services and manufacturing, the UK's share of world exports has fallen. Between 1968 and 1989 the share of manufactured exports fell from 9.6 to 6.4 per cent while the share of world exports of services fell more noticeably from 11.9 to 7.2 per cent. While it is clear that exports of services do make an important contribution to the current account, it is unlikely that the growth of exports necessary to *raise* the rate of growth of output consistent with balance of payments equilibrium can be provided by the service sector. Exports of manufactured goods are more important in terms of their contribution to the value of total UK exports and in terms of growth, both actual and potential. This contribution will become increasingly important as earnings from oil exports decline over the next twenty years, and as international trade in services becomes more intense.

Conclusion

As a conclusion to this chapter we can do no better than reproduce selected quotations from the recent House of Lords Select Committee on Science and Technology (see the reading list and pages 22/23):

- 'We must have a concerted campaign to promote greater esteem for manufacturing industry.'
- 'Government must lead this campaign and proclaim the central position of manufacturing to out national prosperity.'
- 'All the evidence shows that the present lack of government commitment, support and assistance is deeply damaging to industry and to our national interest. We are confident that the changes we recommend would contribute significantly to restoring a better balance between the two extremes of government policy.'
- 'Only a substantial increase in manufacturing output can correct the huge deficit on our balance of trade.'
- 'Action is needed now to stop the decline of our manufacturing industry.'
- 'The most urgent need is for a change in our culture. Unless we revise radically some of the attitudes which permeate our society we will continue to be neglected. Antipathy to manufacturing industry runs deep in our society.'

KEY WORDS

Unemployment	Vicious circle
Economic growth	Balance of payments
Kaldor's Growth Laws	Visible balance
Gross domestic product	Invisible balance
Static increasing returns to scale	Constrained growth
Dynamic increasing returns	Equilibrium growth rate
Disguised unemployment	Elasticity
Diminishing returns	Exports of services
Virtuous circle of growth	

Reading list

'Deindustrialization: Does it matter?', *Economic Affairs*, April/May 1989.

Eatwell, J., Chapter 3 in *Whatever Happened to Britain?* Duckworth, 1982.

Healey, N. and Levačić, R., Chapter 2 in *Supply Side Economics*, 2nd edn, Heinemann Educational, 1992.

House of Lords, *Report of the Select Committee on Science and Technology: Innovation in Manufacturing Industries*, HMSO, 1991.

Paisley, R. and Quillfeldt, J., Exercise 25 in *Economics Investigated*, Collins Educational, 1989.

Thirlwall, A.P. and Gibson, H.D., Chapter 12 in *Balance of Payments Theory and the United Kingdom Experience*, 4th edn, Macmillan, 1992.

Essay topics

1. Discuss the main causes of Britain's economic growth performance in recent years. Is growth necessary, or desirable, in your opinion? (Joint Matriculation Board, 1989)

2. What are the main sources of economic growth? Why has the UK consistently recorded a growth performance below that of other major European economies? (Combined boards of Oxford & Cambridge/ Southern Universities/Cambridge Local, AS-level, 1990)

Data Response Question 3

Growth in labour productivity in the group of seven industrial countries, 1960–88

This task is based on a question set by Oxford and Cambridge Schools Examination Board/University of Cambridge Local Examinations Syndicate (at AS-level) in 1991. Study Table A which has data from *Economic Progress Report*, April 1989. Answer the following questions.

1. (i) Explain what you understand by 'productivity'. (ii) The table shows international comparisons of productivity changes for the whole economy and manufacturing industry. Which set of data would you expect to be more valid and why?
2. (i) Which country has experienced the highest overall increase in productivity since 1960? (ii) Which country has experienced the highest overall increase in productivity growth between the 1970s and 80s?
3. Which country seems to have experienced the lowest rate of productivity increase in its *non-manufacturing* sector from 1980–88? Justify your answer.
4. (i) State two factors which might influence the average annual change in labour productivity in an economy. (ii) Explain how the two factors you have identified might explain international variations shown in the table.
5. *For the UK*, comment upon the likely internal and external implications of the productivity changes shown in the table.

Table A Output per person employed (average annual % changes)

	1960–70	1970–80	1980–88
Whole economy			
United Kingdom	2.4	1.3	2.5
USA	2.0	0.4	1.2
Japan	8.9	3.8	2.9
West Germany	4.4	2.8	1.8
France	4.6	2.8	2.0
Italy	6.3	2.6	2.0
Canada	2.4	1.5	1.4
Manufacturing industry			
United Kingdom	3.0	1.6	5.2
USA	3.5	3.0	4.0
Japan	8.8	5.3	3.1
West Germany	4.1	2.9	2.2
France	5.4	3.2	3.1
Italy	5.4	3.0	3.5
Canada	3.4	3.0	3.6

Chapter Four
The causes of deindustrialization since 1966

There are factors that make the income elasticity of demand for UK exports of manufactured goods low, and the income elasticity of imports high.

There have been four main views put forward to explain the process of deindustrialization:

- technical progress
- the Bacon–Eltis thesis
- the impact of North Sea oil, and
- the weak trade performance of the UK manufacturing sector.

Each of them purports to explain the long-term decline in manufacturing employment. In assessing these views, we shall also look at wider evidence to check their consistency.

Technical progress
Technical progress is claimed to have led to capital displacing labour in the production process. We know from the concept of the **production function**, which relates output to inputs, that labour and capital are used together to produce output. In explaining deindustrialization, it is claimed that technical progress has been of a labour-saving nature.

In Figure 6 we have plotted trends for the capital stock, employment and output in manufacturing for the period 1966–90. It is clear that the capital stock has grown fairly smoothly while the trend in employment is downwards, although with cyclical variations. Manufacturing output also follows a cyclical pattern: growing up to 1973; then falling to a low in the slump of 1979–82; then rising to a new peak in 1989.

Since the capital stock is fixed in the short run, it is employment that adjusts to cyclical fluctuations in output. However, it is not possible to

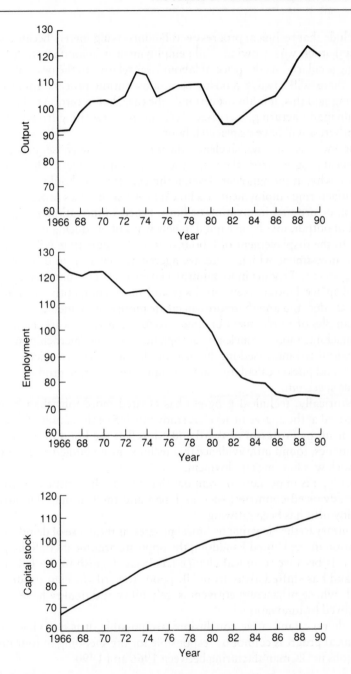

Figure 6 Trends in output, employment and capital between 1966 and 1990 (indexed to 1980 = 100)

conclude that technical progress was labour-saving merely because the capital stock was growing while employment in manufacturing was falling secularly. As the price of labour rises relative to the price of capital, there will always tend to be a substitution process going on. Having said this, it is almost certainly the case that in certain industries within manufacturing, increased mechanization resulting from technical progress will have displaced labour.

But one must distinguish clearly the *microeconomic* consequences of technical progress from the *macroeconomic* consequences. There is no reason why, at the aggregate level, technical progress should mean *less* manufacturing employment. Technical progress involves process innovation or product innovation or both. **Process innovation** at a given level of output, involving capital in new ways of producing things, will lead to the displacement of labour, but at the same time will involve more investment which increases aggregate demand (and therefore employment). **Product innovation** at a given level of output may or may not displace labour. New products and more competitive products increase demand and therefore can create more employment.

Examples of employment-creating product innovations are the washing machine, motor vehicle and aeroplane; while the microchip, which has permitted increased mechanization, has also created micro-computers and pocket calculators and has improved existing products over a wide spectrum.

Historically, technical progress has created more jobs than it has destroyed at the aggregate level. A study in 1985 of the causes of unemployment, by Professors Layard and Nickell at the London School of Economics, found little evidence that technology embodied in the capital stock was limiting employment.

Finally, it is important to point out that even in the most technologically advanced countries, such as Japan and the US, manufacturing employment has been growing.

Contrary to the view that technical progress is the cause of deindustrialization in the United Kingdom, the opposite argument could be put that it is because technical change has been *sluggish* in the UK that demand has shifted away from UK goods towards foreign-produced goods whose price competitiveness, reliability and quality have been improved by innovation.

While no quantitative conclusions are possible, it is our view that technical progress cannot be responsible for the shedding of four million jobs in UK manufacturing between 1966 and 1990.

The Bacon and Eltis thesis

A more detailed account of deindustrialization has been offered by the Oxford economists, Bacon and Eltis, in a controversial book published in 1976 entitled *Britain's Economic Problem: Too Few Producers*. On the basis of a wealth of evidence, they claim that the increased proportion of resources devoted to those public sector activities that do not market their output (including loss-making nationalized industries) has *crowded out* resources available to the manufacturing and other sectors that do market their output.

Their thesis can be illustrated in various ways using the national income accounts. *National income from the expenditure side* is equal to the sum of consumption, investment and the balance of payments surplus (exports minus imports). The balance of payments surplus, by definition, is made up of **marketable output**, but consumption and investment may either be in the marketable output or **non-marketable output** sectors. It follows that if there is an increase in the amount of expenditure devoted to non-marketable output, and the consumption of marketable output does not fall, then investment in the marketable output sector and/or the balance of payments must suffer. Or in terms of shares of national income, if the share of expenditure in the non-marketable output sector increases, and the consumption of marketable output does not decline as a proportion of income, then the share of investment plus the trade balance must deteriorate.

National income measured by output is equal to the value-added of non-marketable output goods, marketable consumption goods, marketable investment goods, and the trade balance. If the output of non-marketable goods rises and the output of marketable consumption goods does not fall, then either investment or the balance of payments must suffer.

National income measured by types of income is equal to wages and profits (including dividends, interest, etc.) paid in the production of marketable goods, plus wages and profits paid in the production of non-marketable goods, plus the balance of payments surplus. If the wage bill in the non-marketable output sector rises, through the growth of employment or wage rate increases, then profits in industry and/or the balance of payments will suffer unless wages in the marketable output sector fall. If profits fall, investment in industry will fall.

Bacon and Eltis claim that employment outside the marketable output sector rose by roughly one-third relative to employment in the marketable output sector from 1961 to 1974, apparently far in excess of other countries. Employment in education increased by 76 per cent, local government employment increased by 54 per cent, and central government employment by 10 per cent (all producing non-marketable output). Wages in these occupations also rose in excess of the average, and the effect on the economy as a whole was a fall in profits net of tax to the detriment of investment in the marketable output sector. Had the industrial base been strengthened by more investment in the marketable output sector, deindustrialization would have been considerably reduced and the overall macroeconomic performance of the economy would have been much healthier.

Weaknesses in the argument

There are several weaknesses in the argument. The essential task is to show that non-market activities have starved the manufacturing sector of resources – especially labour and investment funds – which would otherwise have been productively used in manufacturing.

On the labour shortage hypothesis, the Bacon and Eltis argument is not supported by the facts. Between 1966 and 1976, the labour shed by the manufacturing sector was mainly male whereas the labour employed in the public sector was mainly female. The manufacturing sector was not starved of labour by the growth of employment in the public sector. In the 1980s there was a permanent pool of unemployed labour.

As far as investment is concerned, it is possible that the resources required by a growing public sector could have reduced the funds available for profitable investment in the market sector. With labour productivity growing faster than the demand for output, labour will be shed from manufacturing unless there is investment in new and technologically advanced activities. Was there **crowding out** of investment from the private sector?

Table 8 Investment in the UK 1961–89

	Private-sector investment as a percentage of total	Manufacturing investment at 1985 prices (£ million)
1961	62	8 915
1967	53	8 399
1970	58	10 666
1972	62	8 496
1974	58	10 036
1979	71	10 136
1982	74	6 360
1989	85	10 787

Source: *Economic Trends*, Annual Supplement

To examine this argument in more detail, Table 8 shows movements in the proportion of total investment accounted for by the private sector and the level of real manufacturing investment. The years shown represent peaks and troughs in the ratio of private to total investment. In 1961 private investment represented 62 per cent of the total, and by 1967 it had fallen to 53 per cent – the lowest point in the period covered. Up to 1972 it rose gradually to 62 per cent, falling slightly between 1972 and 1974 and then rising to 85 per cent in 1989. If Bacon and Eltis were correct then we would expect a gradual but constant downward trend in the proportion of investment stemming from the private sector. Apart from the period 1961–67 this does not appear to be the case. Perhaps more important is the fall in real manufacturing investment after 1970 – which picked up after 1972 before falling dramatically after 1979 and did not regain its 1970 level until 1989. This cannot be attributed to government claims on investment funds which were declining in relative terms from 1974 onwards.

In the light of the evidence, it is hard to sustain the view that the growth of the non-market sector has been a cause of deindustrialization.

North Sea oil

Another explanation of the more recent demise of manufacturing industry concerns the discovery and export of North Sea oil. The argument is as follows.

Theory

Consider a small open economy such as the UK with two sectors: one sector producing goods which are traded internationally (which we assume to be the manufacturing sector) and a sector producing non-traded goods (assumed to be the service sector). Further assume that all factors of production are fully employed and mobile between sectors. The price P_t of tradeable goods relative to the price P_n of non-tradeables measured in a common currency is

$$P_t/P_n = eP_w/P_n,$$

where P_w is the world price of tradeables (measured, say, in US dollars) and e is the exchange rate measured as the domestic (sterling) price of dollars. Since the world price of traded goods is assumed fixed, the relative price of traded goods can only change if the exchange rate changes, or if the price of non-traded goods changes.

Now consider Figure 7 which shows the supply of exports and demand for imports in relation to the relative price of tradeables. At P_0

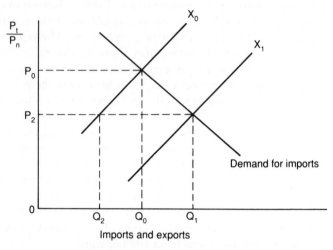

Figure 7 The supply of exports and demand for imports in relation to the relative price of tradeables

the balance of payments is in equilibrium. This equilibrium is then disturbed by the discovery and export of oil. The supply of exports curve shifts to the right (X_0 to X_1) since more exports will be forthcoming at a given relative price of traded goods. If the demand for imports remains constant (the full-employment assumption), then the relative price of traded goods falls to P_2 in order to establish a new equilibrium. This happens through the process of exchange rate appreciation (i.e. a fall in the sterling price of dollars). It can be seen, therefore, that in a static framework with the full employment of resources and flexible prices, the introduction of oil exports reduces the output of manufactured goods if the balance of payments is to remain in equilibrium. At P_2, exports of manufactured goods fall to OQ_2, with Q_2–Q_1 representing oil exports.

The facts
On the surface, this theoretical account of deindustrialization would seem to fit the facts of the late 1970s when oil production increased rapidly along with exports of fuels. As Table 9 shows, the extraction of North Sea oil (and gas) began in earnest in 1976 and grew rapidly thereafter, and by 1983 the volume of fuel exports was four times higher than in 1975. The effective exchange rate (i.e. the exchange rate relative to a basket of currencies), however, did not begin to appreciate until 1978, when fuel exports rose by 43 per cent in one year,

Table 9 The impact of North Sea oil (1980 = 100)

	Output of gas and oil	Fuel exports	Fuel imports	Effective sterling exchange rate
1975	0.3	33	150	104.1
1976	16.2	40	151	89.1
1977	47.4	55	125	84.6
1978	68.9	70	121	84.9
1979	98.7	100	119	90.0
1980	100.0	100	100	100.0
1981	110.3	121	82	98.9
1982	125.6	123	75	94.2
1983	137.6	148	67	86.7
1984	147.1	160	87	81.9
1985	150.3	171	86	81.8
1986	153.1	175	94	75.9
1987	149.2	173	95	75.7
1988	138.8	174	102	68.1
1989	110.8	181	105	59.0
1990	111.5	179	117	58.0

Sources: *Monthly Digest of Statistics* (various)

suggesting that the impact of oil on the manufacturing sector could not have occurred until the very late 1970s.

There are, however, shortcomings in the theoretical model. There is nothing inevitable about a fall in the relative price of traded goods following a natural-resource discovery which earns foreign exchange. There are a number of ways in which additional foreign exchange can be used which would keep the relative price of tradeables at P_0 by preventing the exchange rate appreciating:

- it could be accumulated;
- it could be invested abroad;
- it could be used to buy more imports as part of a process of expansion, especially if the economy is not at full employment; or
- it could be invested as part of a growth strategy.

How the exchange rate moves is at the discretion of the monetary authorities. The fact that the exchange rate was allowed to rise in 1979 undoubtedly contributed to the contraction of manufacturing industry; but it was not the *inevitable* result of North Sea oil. In any case, the process of deindustrialization began in the 1960s, and as a long-term trend it has nothing to do with the recent exploitation of North Sea oil.

If we consider long-run trends, a more convincing explanation lies in the weak trade performance of the UK manufacturing sector, particularly the slow growth of exports relative to the propensity to import, as outlined in the model earlier.

The weak trade performance

The importance of manufacturing industry for the UK balance of payments has already been emphasized above. The balance of trade in

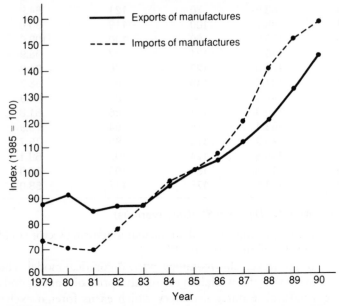

Figure 8 Exports and imports of manufactures 1979–1990 (1985 = 100)

Table 10 Balance of trade in manufactured goods (£million)

	Exports	Imports	Balance
1979	30 950	28 240	+2 710
1980	34 877	29 449	+5 428
1981	34 898	30 401	+4 497
1982	37 314	35 220	+2 094
1983	40 149	42 881	−2 732
1984	46 555	51 082	−4 527
1985	52 240	56 005	−3 765
1986	54 436	60 561	−6 125
1987	60 651	68 763	−8 112
1988	64 912	80 012	−15 100
1989	75 478	92 300	−16 822

manufactured goods has traditionally been in surplus, but the surplus has been gradually eroded since the mid-1960s. In 1965, the value of exports of manufactured goods was more than 180 per cent of the value of imports, and by 1974 it had fallen to less than 120 per cent. Since then the trend has continued downwards with fluctuations towards the point where, in 1983, there was for the first time in history a deficit on the **balance of trade** in manufactured goods (see Figure 8 and Table 10).

It is the weak trade performance of the manufacturing sector, reflected in the gradual elimination of the trade surplus, that provides the most convincing explanation of deindustrialization – measured in terms of the absolute, long-term decline in employment in the manufacturing sector. The fact is that UK manufacturers have not been able to sell enough, either at home or abroad, for the growth of output in manufacturing to exceed the growth of labour productivity, and inevitably employment has decreased. Exports have not grown fast enough, and imported manufactured goods have steadily penetrated the UK market, as shown by the trends in Figure 8.

Import penetration

To analyse the problem in more detail, Table 11 shows how **import penetration** – which reduces the growth of UK manufacturers' sales in the UK – has risen since 1977. In aggregate, foreign producers increased their share of the UK market for manufactured goods from 25 per cent in 1977 to nearly 37 per cent in 1989, an increase of 50 per cent in twelve years. Sectors experiencing large increases in import penetration were chemicals and man-made fibres, electrical and electronic engineering, motor vehicles, textiles, and leather goods.

Table 12 shows exports as a proportion of manufacturers' sales for the period 1977–89. On the whole, the export record has not been good, with the share of export sales rising only 4.3 percentage points in twelve years. Even this increase is deceptive since increased import penetration has reduced the growth of home sales (and therefore the growth of total sales) of UK manufacturers, thus introducing bias into export performance when it is measured by the *share* of exports in total sales. Overall, there can be no doubt that the trade performance of the UK manufacturing sector has worsened considerably since 1968, and this is reflected in the gradual elimination of the trade surplus since the mid-1960s, while manufacturing employment has fallen and unemployment has grown.

Table 11 Import penetration in the UK: Imports as a percentage of home demand

	1977	1983	1989
Total manufacturing	25.1	31.1	36.7
Metals	32	36	17
Other minerals & mineral products	12	13	-
Chemicals & man-made fibres	27	36	42
Metal goods n.e.s.	9	13	18
Mechanical engineering	30	32	40
Office machinery & data processing equipment	84	106	95
Electrical & electronic engineering	30	42	52
Motor vehicles & parts	35	52	51
Other transport equipment	45	42	49
Instrument engineering	51	55	60
Food, drink & tobacco	17	17	18
Textile industry	27	41	48
Leather & leather goods	32	44	52
Clothing & footwear	25	33	40
Timber & wooden furniture	28	32	30
Paper, printing & publishing	21	20	22
Rubber & plastics processing	17	24	26
Other manufacturing industries	34	38	45

Source: *Annual Abstract of Statistics*, 1991

Table 12 Exports as a percentage of manufacturers' sales

	1977	1983	1989
Total manufacturing	25.7	26.6	30.0
Metals	22	25	-
Other minerals & mineral products	17	14	16
Chemicals & man-made fibres	35	42	47
Metal goods n.e.s.	14	12	13
Mechanical engineering	44	40	39
Office machinery & data processing equipment	80	110	93
Electrical & electronic engineering	37	37	46
Motor vehicles & parts	42	37	33
Other transport equipment	47	55	60
Instrument engineering	50	51	54
Food, drink & tobacco	9	10	12
Textile industry	27	28	32
Leather & leather goods	27	33	41
Clothing & footwear	19	18	19
Timber & wooden furniture	7	6	4
Paper, printing and publishing	11	10	10
Rubber & plastics processing	22	22	20
Other manufacturing industries	37	28	30

Source: *Annual Abstract of Statistics*, 1991

Increasing deficit with the EC

A further dimension of the problem is revealed in Table 13, which shows the balance of trade in manufactured goods with various blocs of countries. The most noticeable feature in the pattern of trade is the increasing deficit with countries in the European Community (EC) since 1973, the year in which the UK joined. In 1970, the UK had a balance of trade surplus in manufactured goods with each bloc listed in Table 13 except with North America. By 1974 the UK had a trade deficit with each bloc except for 'other countries'. Throughout the 1980s the situation continued to worsen, but more so with the EC than elsewhere. Only the recession caused the deficit with the EC to fall from £11 billion in 1987 to £10 billion in 1990.

Table 13 UK balance of trade in manufactures with other blocs of countries 1970–90 (£million)

	European Community	Other Western Europe	North America	Other countries
1970	+164	+457	−210	+1861
1972	−80	+285	+222	+1716
1974	−646	−50	−222	+2675
1976	−463	+295	−176	+4734
1978	−1615	−784	−147	+6464
1980	−1764	−182	−1465	+6979
1982	−4983	−1028	−1362	+7574
1984	−8350	−2439	−1153	+5544
1987	−11085	−2796	−1398	+5333
1990	−9929	−3191	−2050	+1258

Source: *Overseas Trade Statistics* (various years)

What accounts for the overall weak trade performance of the UK manufacturing sector?

An obvious approach is to look at why the demand for UK manufactured goods at home and abroad has been relatively weak. In the foregoing analysis it was noted that demand depends on relative prices and income. A low demand for UK-produced goods may result, therefore, from a high relative price via the price elasticity of demand and/or a low income elasticity of demand in the presence of rising real income. The cause of the problem can therefore be analysed in terms, on the one hand, of **price competitiveness** and, on the other hand, the factors which make UK goods less desirable to consumers when their income rises.

Relative unit labour costs

Much emphasis has been placed on price uncompetitiveness as the reason for the poor trade performance of the UK manufacturing sector. This assertion is usually supported by a list of factors that have contributed to increased costs – such as trade union militancy, low productivity, inefficient management, low investment, high exchange rates and uncoordinated industrial policy. Each of these factors will contribute to increased costs, but first it is necessary to show that over a long period there has been a progressive reduction in price or cost competitiveness.

We need to look at the costs or prices of UK manufactured goods relative to those of other countries (with adjustment for exchange rate changes). A common measure of competitiveness is the **IMF index of relative unit labour costs,** which is shown for the period 1963–89 (along with **relative producer prices**) in Figure 9. Producer prices incorporate costs other than labour costs and may be a more representative index of competitiveness. An increase in either index represents a reduction in competitiveness as the cost of UK goods rises relative to the cost of foreign goods.

In fact, between 1963 and 1976, the indices move in parallel on a *downward* trend. The competitiveness of UK products was improving, although not continuously. Following the effects of the 1967 devaluation, between 1968 and 1971 the indices rose but not back to their original levels. However, by 1976 both indices indicate that competitiveness had improved by over 20 per cent since 1966. From 1976 to 1981, competitiveness then deteriorated dramatically as a result of rapid wage inflation and later currency appreciation, but after the early

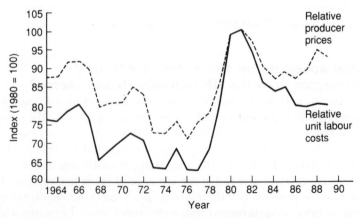

Figure 9 Measures of competitiveness 1963–89

1980s competitiveness improved and is no worse today than at the beginning of the 1960s. Thus, as an explanation of the downward trend in the trade surplus in manufactured goods, the cost competitiveness argument is difficult to sustain.

Income elasticity of demand

But, in any case, competitiveness is not the only determinant of the demand for goods. What is happening to income, and the characteristics of goods, are also very important. If income increases, demand will increase if the product in question is a 'normal' good. According to the concept of the **income elasticity of demand**, we can distinguish between 'necessities', where the income elasticity of demand is less than one (so that a 1 per cent increase in income is associated with an increase in demand of *less* than 1 per cent), and 'luxuries', where the income elasticity of demand is greater than one. A declining trade surplus in manufactured goods with improved competitiveness could occur if the goods produced by UK manufacturers in general possess a low income elasticity of demand, while those produced by competitors have a higher income elasticity.

Given that the balance of trade in manufactured goods has not moved in the expected direction when competitiveness improved means that increases in income in the UK and abroad, combined with the income elasticity of demand, must have had an important impact. *It is to the factors that make the income elasticity of demand for UK exports of manufactured goods low, and the income elasticity of imports high, that we must look for the explanation of Britain's deteriorating trade performance in manufacturing.*

Non-price factors

Research undertaken by the National Economic Development Office (NEDO) points to the importance of **non-price factors** which have rendered UK manufactured goods in general less desirable. Non-price competitiveness, which affects the income elasticity of demand, concerns such factors as: product quality and reliability, the standard of after-sales service, and delivery. The important determinants of non-price competitiveness are therefore expenditure on research and development (R and D) and the way in which products are marketed.

Yet to gauge the actual degree of non-price competitiveness is difficult. How is the quality of a product measured, for instance?

D. Connell (consult the reading list) argues that a purchaser chooses between goods on the basis of value for money and not simply on the basis of relative prices. If products are homogeneous there should, in the long term, be no differences in price and so prices must diverge for reasons of product heterogeneity. If this is so, then it would be expected that products of better quality or technologically superior would have a higher value per tonne.

Connell found that in 1975 West German manufacturers were earning around 60 per cent more per tonne from exports of mechanical engineering products than were British manufacturers, and he attributes this to non-price factors. In addition to this, he found that UK manufacturing firms 'have treated exporting as a marginal activity, rather than integrating it fully into their operations', and operate mainly in the smaller, slow-growing international markets.

Testing theories of deindustrialization

Read the accompanying article from *The Times* of 2 December 1981 and the letter published in that newspaper on 11 December 1981. Answer the following questions.

1. Which of the five theories put forward to account for deindustrialization relate to the long-term trend and which to the recent experience?
2. Is 'stupid' a fair description of some of the economic policies pursued by government which have contributed to deindustrialization? Think of a defence.
3. Why does the Bacon and Eltis explanation of deindustrialization fail to explain the experience of the last decade?
4. What is wrong with the explanation that North Sea oil must cause an absolute contraction of manufacturing output and employment?
5. What do you understand by the 'New Cambridge' explanation of deindustrialization?
6. David Blake does not mention technical progress as a cause of deindustrialization. Do you think this is a mistake?
7. Can employment in service activities substitute for a decline in jobs in manufacturing?

Deindustrialization – testing theories

The huge drop in manufacturing output – down by more than a sixth since spring 1979 – has been the most striking feature of the recession. But in the debate about the Government's macroeconomic policies of the past two years, we often lose sight of the fact that the decline in manufacturing is not new.

It has been a persistent feature of the last eight years. In the mid-1970s it was identified by left and right as one of the country's prime economic problems. Many theories were put forward to explain why it was happening.

If we are to understand what is going on and what we ought to do about it, we ought to look again at some longer term explanations which have been put forward for what is going on in the industrial sector.

There are five main explanations of what has been happening which we should consider.

One is that the problems have been caused by stupid economic policies by the Government, which drove up the exchange rate through high interest rates, incited big pay rises by its tax policy and deflated the domestic economy by cutting its borrowing requirement.

Then there is the North Sea explanation, first put forward by Kay and Forsyth, which says that North Sea oil automatically causes a contraction in manufacturing output.

A third explanation is that of Bacon and Eltis, that growth of the public sector has led to contraction of manufacturing. The fourth is what is usually called the "New Cambridge" explanation, that growing imports eat up the British market and that conventional solutions, such as devaluation, will not stop this. Only import controls can meet the challenge under this scenario.

The fifth explanation is really the mirror image of the first. It says that contraction in manufacturing is a sign that the Government's policies have, at great cost, worked. Useless capacity which had been outdated by the 1973 oil shock has at last been removed and the industrial sector has become more efficient in response to competition.

As an explanation of what has happened in the past two years, the Bacon and Eltis explanation does not work. They argued that the sign of the deindustrialization of Britain was the shift of workers from the trading to the public sector. By pre-empting resources the Government was effectively "crowding out" the private sector. Yet public employment has not risen in the past two years; it has fallen.

The million jobs lost in manufacturing have not been to the benefit of extra public service jobs; they have resulted in an increase in unemployment. Bacon and Eltis themselves warned that what was needed was not to cut the public sector but to boost the trading sector.

They wrote: "there would be the certainty of disaster if a Conservative pro-market sector government came to power and just sat back, balanced the budget and let unemployment mount waiting for the market to solve its problems."

What about the idea that North Sea oil has made a decline in manufacturing output inevitable. The argument rests on the fact that we export to pay for our imports. As we no longer have to pay for imports of oil, we can import more of other things and export less of our own manufactures. The manufacturing sector will therefore decline.

As a long term explanation this seems unsatisfactory. It is true that the share of manufacturing in our national output would fall in those circumstances. But that is no reason why the absolute level should go down.

What we ought to expect, unless the domestic economy was at full capacity, would be that manufacturing would take a smaller share of a larger whole, but would not actually contract.

Oddly enough this inadequate explanation fits well in one respect with the experience of the past two years. One consequence of North Sea oil was to make sterling a more attractive currency. Supporters of the theory could argue that the pound went up in 1979 and 1980 because investors realized that Britain would get improving benefits to the balance of payments until 1985.

Yet the movements of the pound in 1981 hardly bear out the theory. When British interest rates were below world levels in the summer, the pound fell. Now that our interest rates are once again high, sterling is strengthening. This points strongly to the conclusion that the appreciation of the pound in 1980 owed more to British monetary policies than to a structural shift in the balance of payments.

What about the "New Cambridge" schools of thought which ties deindustrialization to rising imports? The problem here is that imports were falling at the same time that manufacturing went through the floor.

As Sir Alec Cairncross pointed out, without accepting the Cambridge diagnosis of what should be done their definition of what deindustrialization means has a lot to commend it. But over the past two years, it does not fit as a description of what has been happening.

Whether the Government was right to do what it did or not is something we can only tell in time; though it if was, it ought to be saying that the future lies with the growth of services, not telling workers to accept low pay settlements to hang on to jobs in manufacturing.

But it is a strange irony that a government whose election owed so much to a feeling that manufacturing had been treated too badly should have presided over the greatest industrial recession this century.

DAVID BLAKE

Loss of jobs in manufacturing

From Professor A.P. Thirlwall
David Blake's article on deindustrialization was timely, but his analysis leaves a misleading impression in some respects. The absolute loss of jobs in manufacturing industry has been a persistent feature not only of the last eight years, but of the last 15.

Employment in manufacturing as a whole peaked in 1966 and has declined progressively by three million since then from nine million to six million, with a loss of one million in the last two years alone. This historical and recent decline is unparalleled in the world.

The argument that the growth of public-sector employment has been responsible for this worrying decline not only fails to explain what has happened in the last two years, but does not stand up to scrutiny over the longer time scale. The "New Cambridge" argument, which ties deindustrialization to the inability of exports to pay for full employment imports, or in other words to a fundamental balance of payments constraint on output, cannot be discounted by saying that the "problem here is that imports were falling at the same time that manufacturing went through the floor".

The depression of imports is itself a function of contraction which may still have had as one of its roots an imbalance between exports and plans to import.

As far as the longer term is concerned, my own work reveals a strong rank correlation across industries between the rate of employment decline and the rate of deterioration in the balance between imports and exports. A long-term solution to deindustrialization requires a foreign trade strategy based on the promotion of exports.

As far as the last two years are concerned, however, David Blake is correct that the loss of jobs can really only be satisfactorily explained in terms of the massive domestically engineered deflation of demand. It was pleasing to read in your same issue that at least one sinner at the London Business School has repented.

Your sincerely,
A.P. THIRLWALL,
Keynes College,
The University,
Canterbury,
Kent

Summary conclusion

It is clear, then, that it is not primarily reduced cost competitiveness that has contributed to the diminution of the UK trade surplus in manufactured goods. In the longer term, it is non-price factors such as design, quality, marketing and other parts of the product package that have contributed to a low income elasticity of demand for UK manufactured goods. The weak trade performance of the UK manufacturing sector has been due more to non-price factors than simply to price uncompetitiveness.

KEY WORDS

Production function	Import penetration
Process innovation	Price competitiveness
Product innovation	IMF index of relative unit
Marketable output	labour costs
Non-marketable output	Relative producer prices
Crowding out	Income elasticity of demand
North Sea oil	Non-price factors
Balance of trade	

Reading list

Bacon, R. and Eltis, W., *Britain's Economic Problem: Too Few Producers*, 2nd edn, Macmillan, 1976.

Clark, A. and Layard, R., *UK Unemployment*, Heinemann Educational, 2nd Edition, 1993.

Connell, D., *The UK's Performance in Export Markets*, NEDO Discussion Paper 6, 1979

Smith, C., *UK Trade and Sterling*, Heinemann Educational, 1992.

Essay topics

1. Analyse the main trends in employment in UK manufacturing industry since 1960. Discuss the main causes of these changes. (Combined boards of Oxford & Cambridge/Southern Universities/ Cambridge Local, AS-level, 1990)

2. What is meant by 'technical progress' and how does it affect the efficiency of an industry? How does government policy influence the rate of technical progress in the UK? (Joint Matriculation Board, AS-level, 1990)

3. 'The riches of North sea oil – over £100 billion in tax revenues alone – could have been used to transform Britain's economy. Instead, they have been squandered'. Do you agree? (Oxford & Cambridge Schools Examination Board, 1992)

Data Response Question 4

Study the data in the tables below and then answer the questions which follow.

Table 1 Distribution of the workforce

Thousands

	1979	1983	1986	1989
Employees in employment:				
Manufacturing	7 253	5 252	5 227	5 191
Services	13 580	13 501	14 297	15 427
Other	2 340	2 024	1 863	1 835
Self-employed persons	1 906	2 221	2 627	2 986
Unemployed	1 312	3 127	3 312	1 842

(From: *Annual Abstract of Statistics* 1990 edition *Social Trends* (20) 1990 edition)

Table 2 Gross domestic product at current prices

£ million

	1979	1983	1986	1988
Whole economy	172 804	260 399	324 031	394 787
Manufacturing	48 714	61 299	76 485	93 433

(From: *Annual Abstract of Statistics* 1990 edition)

Table 3 Output per person employed

Index numbers 1985 = 100

	1979	1983	1986	1988
Whole economy	89.1	96.7	102.9	107.4
Manufacturing	79.9	91.8	103.1	115.7

(From: *Economic Trends Annual Supplement* 1990 edition)

Table 4 Visible trade of the United Kingdom

	1979	1983	1986	1988
Volume index numbers				
1985 = 100				
Exports	83.1	87.6	104.0	110.7
Imports	83.5	87.0	107.1	129.5
Value (£ million)				
Visible balance	−3 344	−1 509	−9 364	−20 826

(From: *Annual Abstract of Statistics* 1990 edition)

(a) (i) Describe the main changes in the distribution of the United Kingdom's workforce between 1979 and 1989, as shown in Table 1.

   (ii) Examine the possible causes of the changes you have described.

(b) To what extent do the data support the view that the United Kingdom economy has gone through a period of de-industrialization?

(c) Discuss the significance of the changes which have occurred in United Kingdom manufacturing industry for the performance of the economy.

(Associated Examining Board, 1992)

Chapter Five

The collapse of the manufacturing sector after 1979

'... deindustrialization has produced serious structural imbalances in the British economy.'   M. Kirby

We pointed out in Chapter 1 that employment in manufacturing industry peaked in 1966, and since then it has been on a downward trend. In 1979, the Conservatives under Mrs Thatcher were elected to power after five years of Labour government, and Britain became a laboratory experiment for the application of the doctrine of **monetarism.** Very tight monetary and fiscal policy was pursued in order to 'squeeze inflation out of the system'.

Inflation did eventually abate, but the price was the deepest recession since the great depression of the early 1930s. The contraction of the manufacturing sector between 1979 and 1982 was unprecedented. Output fell by 16 per cent, investment fell by over 30 per cent, 1.3 million jobs were lost, and unemployment in the economy as a whole rose from 1.3 million to 2.8 million. There was some recovery from 1983, and an economic boom from 1987 to 1989, after which there was another deep recession with manufacturing output falling by 10 per cent from 1989 to 1991 and manufacturing employment falling by 7 per cent.

In this chapter, we first of all examine the factors that led to the collapse of the manufacturing sector at the beginning of the 1980s, and then go on to consider why the manufacturing sector continues in what appears to be an inexorable long-run decline.

Explanations of the collapse

Figure 10 gives details of employment and output by sector over the period 1977–90. The indexed statistics show clearly that collapse of manufacturing output and employment was the main feature of the recession of the early 1980s. There was some decline in output and employment in the service sector, but this was relatively small. If the loss of jobs in manufacturing between 1979 and 1983 had continued at

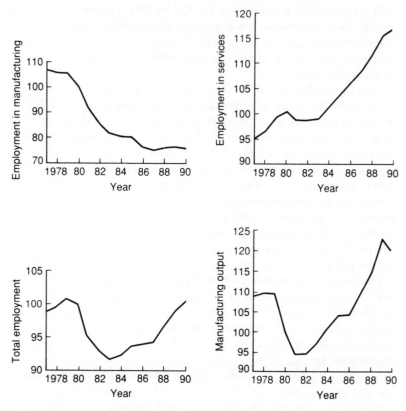

Figure 10 Trend lines for employment and output 1977–90
(indexed to 1980 = 100)

the rate experienced between 1966 and 1979 (when about 150 000
jobs per annum were lost), employment in the manufacturing sector in
1983 would have stood at 6.5 million. The *actual* figure for that year
was 5.5 million. What happened in the early 1980s was not simply a
continuation of past trends but an economic **shock**.

What are the explanations of this shock?

One popular view is that British manufacturing suffered unduly from
the onset of **world recession** around about this time. The argument goes
that for a long period manufacturing in the UK was inefficient, uncom-
petitive and over-manned. The world recession then forced a once-and-
for-all shakeout of inefficient firms, and it is this which caused productivity in British industry to rise by 20 per cent between 1980 and 1983,

and for relative unit labour costs to fall by 14 per cent over the same period. Such a *catharsis*, it was argued, was necessary, and that out of the ashes a phoenix would rise with British industry leaner and fitter, and better equipped to survive in an increasingly competitive international environment.

Does this explanation of events stand up to empirical scrutiny? There is no doubt that there was a severe world recession in the early 1980s. In 1980 world industrial production was stagnant, and during 1981 and 1982 it fell by 10 per cent. A close look at the timing of events in the UK, however, reveals that the collapse of the manufacturing sector was not *initiated* by the world recession. Recessions get transmitted from one country to another through the impact on trade, but the *volume* of world trade in manufactures continued to rise up to 1981 *after* manufacturing output in the UK had declined by some 14 per cent. The world recession exacerbated the decline in output and employment after 1980, but the explanation of the collapse of manufacturing industry lies in factors affecting the UK manufacturing sector *before* 1980.

The first point to mention is that in the two years prior to 1979 there was a sharp deterioration in the balance of trade in manufactured goods to the tune of 17 per cent. The *volume* of imported manufactured goods rose by 25 per cent, while the *volume* of exports remained static. Manufacturing output increased by less than 0.5 per cent. As Professor Chrystal of the London Business School has pointed out (consult the reading list), UK manufacturers were being squeezed out of the domestic market; instead of reducing the scale of their operations immediately, they increased their stocks of goods (i.e. inventories), which rose by nearly 20 per cent up to 1980. It seems that they were expecting demand to revive, but this did not happen.

Why did demand remain depressed?

There were two major reasons why the demand for manufactured goods remained depressed in the early 1980s. The first was the pursuit of a highly **deflationary economic policy** by the newly elected Conservative government in 1979.

The aim of the policy

The primary aim of economic policy became the control of inflation which showed signs of accelerating from an already high level with the collapse of incomes policy in 1978–79 under the previous Labour government. Inflation in 1978–79 was running at an annual rate of over 15 per cent, and wages were rising by over 20 per cent. The government's economic strategy involved cutting government expenditure to reduce the size of the government's deficit (or the so-called **Public Sector Borrowing Requirement** or PSBR) in the belief that this would help to curb the growth of the money supply from the supply side. According to monetarist doctrine, 'inflation is always and everywhere a monetary phenomenon' in a causal sense, and a sufficient condition, therefore, for the control of inflation is control of the money supply.

A so-called **Medium Term Financial Strategy** (MTFS) was introduced with the aim of controlling the growth of M3 money down to below 10 per cent. (MTFS also stands for Mrs Thatcher's Financial Squeeze!) At the same time, interest rates were raised to control the demand for money. The average short-term interest rate rose from 11.6 per cent in 1978 to 15.8 per cent in 1979, and the rate was kept high throughout 1981 and 1982. All this had a dramatic effect on the *internal* demand for manufactured goods, particularly through the adverse impact on investment demand which declined by over 30 per cent.

Exchange rate appreciation
The second important factor which depressed the demand for domestically produced manufactured goods was the rapid appreciation of the exchange rate in 1979 and 1980. Against the dollar, the value of sterling rose from $1.92 in 1978 to $2.33 in 1980 – a rise of over 20 per cent. Against a basket of currencies, the value of sterling (i.e. the effective exchange rate) rose by 18 per cent over the same short period (see Figure 11). Three major factors were responsible for this excessive appreciation:

- Firstly, in the late 1970s, increasing amounts of foreign exchange were being saved and earned by the production and export of North Sea oil. Between 1977 and 1979, fuel output doubled and exports increased by over 80 per cent (see Chapter 4 for full details).
- Secondly, high interest rates made sterling assets attractive for foreigners to hold, which added considerably to the demand for sterling.
- Thirdly, the recession (combined with North Sea oil) caused the *balance of payments on current account* to go into surplus – to the tune of over £3 billion in 1980. This added to the demand for sterling relative to the supply; or to look at it another way, weakened the demand for foreign currency relative to the supply.

The effect of the exchange rate appreciation, however, was to switch demand from domestic to overseas suppliers of manufactured goods on a massive scale. There was an alarming increase in import penetration, and the balance of trade surplus in manufactured goods continued to

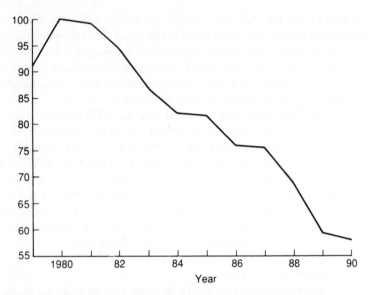

Figure 11 Effective sterling index 1979–90 (1980 = 100)

diminish – until finally in 1983 it went into deficit for the first time in British economic history. The years 1979 to 1981 were an economic nightmare for manufacturing industry. Factories shut down, workers were laid off and the number of bankruptcies and insolvencies rocketed. As Professor Chrystal describes it:

'Domestic firms had lost their grip on the home market. There was no compensating expansion of exports. This increase in import penetration was not due to an upsurge in incompetence on the part of domestic producers. Rather the explanation is found in the fact that this is the period of maximum expansion of North Sea oil.'

Unfavourable long-run trends
As we have argued, however, factors other than North Sea oil, and the impact of oil on the exchange rate, were also at work, including the continuation of unfavourable long-run trends. Indeed, according to econometric work undertaken for the House of Lords Select Committee on Overseas Trade (1985), 'longer term trends' were found to be as important as North Sea oil in accounting for the movement of the balance of trade in manufactures into deficit between 1977 and 1983.

The Select Committee was set up to examine the causes and implications of the deficit on trade in manufactured goods. Looking at the experience of the UK, hearing evidence from interested parties, including industrialists and academics, and examining the experience of other advanced industrial countries, the Committee concluded that the continued decline of the manufacturing sector would 'constitute a grave threat to the standard of living of the British people. Failure to recognize [the] dangers now could have a devastating effect on the future economic and political stability of the nation.' The components of the trade deficit in 1990 are presented in Table 14.

Table 14 Components of the trade deficit in manufactured goods 1990 (£million)

Standard Industrial Trade Classification	Exports (FOB)	Imports (CIF)	Balance of trade
5–8: All manufactured goods	84 202	98 149	−13 947
5: Chemicals & related products	13 181	10 834	+ 2 347
6: Manufactured goods chiefly classified by material, of which:			
64: Paper, paperboard etc.	1 539	4 014	−2 475
65: Textile yarn, fabrics etc.	2 446	3 936	−1 490
7: Machinery and transport equipment of which:			
75: Office machines & automatic data processing equipment	6 341	7 715	−1 374
77: Electrical machinery, apparatus & appliances	5 648	6 921	−1 273
78: Road vehicles	7 296	12 594	−5 298
8: Miscellaneous manufactured goods	13 349	18 252	−4 903

Source: *Overseas Trade Statistics* 1990

Legacy of the collapse

The manufacturing trade balance in deficit, and getting worse, means that Britain's overall growth rate consistent with balance of payments equilibrium on current account is deteriorating; that is, the balance of payments equilibrium growth rate is falling, other things being equal (see Chapter 3). To put it another way, balance of payments deficits will emerge sooner and quicker as growth exceeds a certain level.

This appears to have happened with a vengeance in 1988 and 1989.

With a growth rate of GDP in 1988 of 4.5 per cent, and in 1989 of only 2 per cent, the current account of the balance of payments swung from balance in 1986 to a deficit of £19 billion in 1989. The long-run growth of GDP consistent with payments balance appears to be no more than 2 per cent a year, compared with nearly 3 per cent in the period 1951–79.

LETTER TO THE *FINANCIAL TIMES*, 5 JULY 1988

Current account deficit on the UK balance of payments does matter

From Professor A.P. Thirlwall

Every time I open the Financial Times I read Mr Samuel Brittan* saying that Britain's current account deficit on the balance of payments does not matter, apparently on the grounds that it is being financed voluntarily by capital inflows. The current account deficit does matter, for two main reasons.

First, interest rates are higher than they otherwise would be. This has implications for investment and the modernity of the capital stock. To say that interest rates should be fixed at whatever level is necessary to restrain demand in order to "ensure that the current deficit is held at whatever the capital markets are willing to finance" seems to me to be quite irresponsible. It shows complete indifference to the level of output and employment.

Second, it is certainly true, as Mr Brittan says, that there is no law which states that all countries have to grow at the same rate. There is a law, however, which says that every country will have a growth rate consistent with balance of payments equilibrium, and if growth exceeds that rate payments deficits will emerge.

Since the war, the UK has had the lowest growth rate consistent with balance of payments equilibrium of any major industrial country – which is why the UK has slipped from being one of the richest European countries to one of the poorest.

This may not worry Samuel Brittan, but it worries a lot of other people. General indifference to the structural determinants of the current account of the balance of payments, and in particular to its components, has been a major cause of the deindustrialisation of the UK, with the consequences this has had for the loss of jobs and unemployment. Not until there is concern with the determinants of the current account, and particularly the balance of trade in manufactures, is there any hope of raising the growth rate consistent with balance of payment equilibrium, and reducing unemployment.

Samuel Brittan and the present government may put their faith in market forces, but there is precious little evidence, judging from the balance of payment figures, that the pursuit of laissez-faire for the last nine years has made any difference to the long-run underlying growth rate of the British economy consistent with payments equilibrium.

Lumping the capital and current account of the balance of payments together, and saying there is no problem because the balance of payments must always balance, is to bury one's head in the sand as far as the functioning of the real economy is concerned.

A.P. THIRLWALL
Keynes College,
University of Kent,
Canterbury, Kent
* see page 60

It was fashionable in the 1980s not to regard the size of the deficit as a cause for concern (the letter reproduced on page 58 argues otherwise). Foreigners, it was said, are prepared to finance the current account deficit by holding UK financial assets, which create an offsetting surplus on the capital account (net of changes in reserves). Whether this situation can be sustained depends on overseas confidence in the management and performance of the economy. In particular, rising inflation or a currency depreciation will lead to capital losses for foreigners holding UK financial assets unless the rate of interest in the UK is raised to compensate for these losses. Increases in domestic rates of interest, however, restrain investment, which reduces aggregate demand and undermines the future growth prospects of the UK economy. Interest-elastic consumer expenditures may also be reduced, which will reduce aggregate demand further.

If high interest rates are not sufficient to stave off a **sterling crisis** (in which foreigners withdraw their capital from UK assets causing the demand for sterling to fall), then drastic reductions in aggregate demand will be required to reduce imports and bring the current account back into equilibrium. This will in turn lead to higher unemployment. This is exactly what happened in the late 1980s with the base rate raised from 8.5 per cent in 1987 to 15 per cent in 1989, and *real* interest rates kept high in the early 1990s to protect the value of sterling within the quasi-fixed exchange rate mechanism (ERM) of the European Monetary System (EMS) which Britain joined in 1990. Meanwhile, unemployment in 1991 approached 2.5 million, close to the level of the severe recession of the early 1980s. The balance of payments does matter because the interest rate to protect the currency has implications for the real economy.

Coping with unemployment

Unemployment was on a rising trend in the UK throughout the 1970s. In 1970 unemployment stood at 600 000 and had risen to 1.3 million by 1980. By 1982 it had doubled and eventually reached 3.3 million in 1986. It fell to 1.8 million during the boom 1986–89 (although part of the recorded reduction was due to fewer people claiming unemployment and related benefits, rather than fewer people actually looking for work, as a consequence of changes made to how unemployment figures are collected). Since 1989 unemployment has been rising again. In spite of arguments about the exact number of unemployed people, it is clear that the decline of the manufacturing sector has created an unemployment problem that is still to be cured.

Since employment in the manufacturing sector continues to fall, unemployment will only be reduced if other sectors can grow fast

Hysteria on deficits
Samuel Brittan

Until now the UK trade deficit has been mainly a London preoccupation and participants in overseas financial markets have been remarkably uninterested even in discussing it. If, as a result of the hysteria with which these monthly figures are treated by UK commentators, the British talk themselves into a run on sterling, a slump, or both, it will bear the label "all home made".

As an optimist I think the worst will be avoided. But if it is not, the main responsibility will lie with the instant pundits who are stuck in a time warp. They are too lazy even to become acquainted with the reasons why the current balance of payments is not the appropriate indicator either of a country's economic health or of whether it is paying its way.

Disappointments in the trade figures can matter indirectly for two inter-related reasons. They may be a sign of higher than expected domestic inflationary pressures; and if they cause sterling to weaken there is a further direct feedback into the inflation rate.

But just how bad are the trade figures? Readers of my regular "teenagers' guides" will recall the need to look at longer periods than one month and to go by the volume index, excluding both oil and other erratics.

The picture that then emerges is of a half per cent rise in export volume between the first and second quarters of 1989, followed by a 2 per cent rise in the three months up to August. Imports were virtually flat between the first two quarters, but rose by 4 per cent in the period up to August. That period was distorted – how badly we do not know – by dock strikes.

The healthiness or otherwise of the import upswing depends not on the detailed composition of imports, but on the overall movement of savings and investment. But for what the composition is worth, it shows large rises in capital and intermediate goods shipments and smaller increases in consumer goods imports.

Overall, the best guess one can make is that the current payments deficit is not far from £20bn per annum, or 4 per cent of GDP, if the figures are taken at face value. Much of this deficit could, however, turn out to be imaginary.

Imaginary in two respects. The favourable "balancing item" of positive unrecorded net receipts amounted last year to £12bn or six sevenths of the recorded current deficit. It has been running at similar rates for several years in succession. The IMF now admits that one of the biggest contributions to international imbalances is the statistical black hole by which the world appears to have a payments deficit with itself of nearly $90bn a year. The fund now attributes this hole mainly to the under-recording of portfolio investment income – a gap with obvious implications for a country like the UK with substantial overseas assets.

Second, more fundamentally, Britain's net overseas assets have been rising faster than its liabilities throughout the period of supposed deficit. The appreciation in value of overseas assets has offset the increase in liabilities from any current account red ink.

The appropriate criticism of the Chancellor is not that he down-plays the current balance of payments – which he is right to do. It is that he still clutches at straws like the narrow money-supply measure M0, that is, notes and coins.

Last year the IMF sternly lectured the English-speaking countries on their balance of payments deficits. The fund writers now concede that these deficits and surpluses "reflect in part the international implications of fundamental differences among countries in the balance between private saving and investment, resulting, *inter alia*, from different demographic or technological trends. In a world of highly integrated financial markets, these differences naturally give rise to capital movements in the direction of countries with relatively low savings rates and relatively high (risk adjusted) rates of return on capital." There is more joy in heaven over one sinner who repents than 99 righteous men.

When it comes to the UK, the fund supports current government policy despite the payments deficit. It praises a fiscal surplus that is "one of the healthiest among industrial countries." There is no more talk of fiscal tightening, but merely pressure to retain the budget surplus now envisaged for next year.

Source: *Financial Times*, 28 September 1989

Why the balance of payments matters

TONY THIRLWALL

It became fashionable in the 1980s, when Nigel Lawson was Chancellor, to say that the balance of payments does not matter as long as it is not associated with a budget deficit and is voluntarily financed so that a payments deficit is purely a private matter of no public concern.

There is a fundamental fault with this argument. Private agents do not determine the rate of interest, the Government and the Bank of England determine interest rates – and the balance of payments position and associated pressure on the exchange rate are crucial in determining what the nominal and real rate of interest will be.

Interest rates, in turn, affect the functioning of the real economy by influencing the willingness to invest. The state of the balance of payments, therefore, has economic and social repercussions extending far beyond the free choice exercised by economic agents about how much they wish to spend and to borrow from abroad.

Rates were gradually reduced in the early 1980s as the balance of payments improved and inflation was brought under control through the crude weapon of unemployment. But they were raised again from the mid-1980s as the balance of payments plunged into deficit. Since 1982 the virtually continuous rise in *real* interest rates has been the mirror image of the deterioration of the balance of payments position in relation to GDP.

It is difficult to know precisely what damage interest rate oscillations have done to the economy but if Britain had not experienced balance of payments difficulties as soon as growth approached the rates of its competitors and go-stop avoided, the macro-economy would surely be healthier.

It is not coincidental, for example, that in the 1980s the highest real interest rates in post-war history coincided with zero net investment in manufacturing industry. It was more profitable to hold monetary assets than to invest in plant and machinery.

In the history of economic thought, part of the mercantilist argument was that a strong balance of payments would keep interest rates low and benefit the real economy. This was a central element of Keynes's defence of mercantilism in the 1930s.

Today, 'mercantilist' is used as a term of abuse. Like the mercantilists of old, those who stress the importance of the balance of payments for the real economy are accused of being anti-free trade and confusing money and real wealth.

This is unfair. What both the old and latter-day mercantilists recognise is that the short-term rate of interest is a monetary phenomenon and that it can be too high in relation to the needs of growth and full employment.

The rate of interest required for external equilibrium – to finance deficits and/or to stop the currency collapsing – may be way above that required for internal equilibrium, as we have witnessed in the UK, especially during the past three years.

Nominal interest rates have recently come down as a result of the prolonged recession that has dampened inflation and improved the balance of payments by restricting imports. But we are oceans away from simultaneous internal and external equilibrium.

With the Government's commitment to the exchange rate mechanism of the European Monetary System, Britain is now locked into a system not dissimilar to the gold exchange standard of the Bretton Woods era of 1944–1971 – which, ironically, many of the current supporters of the ERM did their best to undermine in the 1960s – or to the pre-1931 gold standard of fixed exchange rates.

What is currently happening in the UK is reminiscent of what Keynes felt about economic policy in the 1920s when, in his polemic against the return to the gold standard at the pre-war parity in 1925, he described monetary policy as 'simply a campaign against the standard of living of the working classes' operating through the 'deliberate intensification of unemployment . ... a policy which the country would never permit if it knew what was being done.'

It is not the magic wand of the ERM that has brought inflation down to 4 per cent, but the chronic unemployment caused by high interest rates that has knocked the stuffing out of the trade union movement. When recovery comes, there is nothing to stop inflation accelerating again and the balance of payments deteriorating. Interest rates will be raised again and the vicious circle of high interest rates, weak investment, recession and rising unemployment will start once more.

Until policies are designed to improve the balance of payments to allow a sustainable growth rate of at least 2.5 per cent, ERM membership will imply continued high interest rates and high unemployment throughout the 1990s. Those who argue that the current account of the balance of payments does not matter must answer the mercantilist charge.

Source: *Observer*, 29 December 1991

enough, unless the size of the labour force falls. In the 1980s, employment rose almost exclusively in the service sector (see Table 15). In particular, sizeable increases in employment occurred in the financial sector, wholesale and retail distribution and in education. Furthermore, while male employment has hardly changed, female employment has increased substantially by nearly 1.5 million. Corresponding to these changes in the industrial and sex composition of employment is the marked increase in part-time work (defined as 30 hours or less per week). Of the 1.5 million jobs created (in net terms) since 1984, more than half have been for part-time workers.

Table 15 Changes in employment in the UK 1984–89 (thousands)

	1984	1989	Change 1984–89	
Total employees in employment	21 238	22 756	+1 518	(+7.1%)
Males	11 888	11 979	+91	(+0.01%)
Females	9 350	10 776	+1 426	(+15.2%)
Agriculture, forestry & fishing	340	300	−40	(−11.8%)
Energy & water supply	616	471	−145	(−23.5%)
Construction	1 037	1 062	+25	(+0.02%)
Manufacturing industry	5 409	5 234	−175	(−3.2%)
Service industries	13 836	15 688	+1 852	(+13.4%)
of which:				
Wholesale & retail distribution	2 958	3 213	+255	(+8.6%)
Hotels & catering	1 010	1 124	+114	(+11.3%)
Banking finance & insurance	1 969	2 675	+706	(+35.8%)
Public admin. & defence	1 602	1 650	+48	(+3.0%)
Education	1 603	1 797	+194	(+12.1%)
Transport & communication	1 341	1 362	+21	(+1.6%)
Other services	699	892	+193	(+27.6%)

Source: *Annual Abstract of Statistics* 1991

To reduce unemployment further requires not only the creation of jobs for those currently seeking work, but also jobs for those entering the labour force in years to come. These will not only include those who have never worked before, but also those who rejoin the labour force as they perceive improvements in employment prospects (this is the so-called **encouraged worker effect**). In addition, if the manufacturing sector and other production industries continue to shed workers, then even more jobs elsewhere will need to be created. An important question, therefore, is to what extent can a sufficient number of jobs be created in the service sector to bring unemployment down to, say, less than one million? Taken together with the earlier argument that economic growth will be constrained by the current account of the balance of payments, the question can be rephrased as: *Can the UK economy recover to and sustain pre-1979 unemployment levels without a recovery of the manufacturing sector in terms of its contribution to trade and its contribution to employment?* We address this issue in the final chapter.

KEY WORDS

Monetarism
Shock
World recession
Deflationary economic policy
Public Sector Borrowing
   Requirement

Medium Term Financial
   Strategy
Exchange rate
Sterling crisis
Encouraged worker effect

Reading list

Anderton, R., 'Current account of the balance of payments', *Economic Review*, vol. 6, Jan. 1989.

Godley, W., 'The British economy during the Thatcher era', *Journal of the Economics Association*, winter 1989.

Healey, M., 'Do current account deficits matter?', *Economic Review*, March 1991.

Smith, D., *Mrs Thatcher's Economics: Her Legacy*, 2nd edn, Heinemann Educational, 1992.

Thirlwall, A.P., 'The balance of payments and economic performance', *National Westminster Bank Quarterly Review*, May 1992.

Turner, P., 'Change in the pattern of UK trade', *Economic Review*, vol. 5, Jan. 1988.

Essay topics

1. In the 1980s, both national output and the level of unemployment rose in the UK. Examine the possible economic explanations of this phenomenon. (Associated Examining Board, 1987)

2. During the 1980s, the UK's balance of trade in manufactured goods moved from surplus into deficit. Explain why and discuss whether it matters. (Associated Examining Board, 1989)
3. Why has there been a high average level of unemployment in the UK in the 1980s? (University of Oxford Delegacy of Local Examinations, 1989)

Data Response Question 5

Productivity and the trade balance

This task is based on a question set by the Joint Matriculation Board in 1990. Study Tables A–C and Figure A (on page 65) and answer the following questions.

1. Using the data provided, compare the level of growth of productivity in the UK with that of other economies.
2. To what extent do the data support the relationship you would expect to exist in theory between changes in productivity and foreign trade?
3. How might government policies to help the UK's balance of payments position influence trends in UK productivity?
4. Discuss whether the benefits for the United Kingdom of the Single European Market are likely to exceed the costs. (Associated Examining Board, 1992)

Table A Output per person employed (average annual % changes)

	Whole economy			Manufacturing industry		
	1960–70	1970–80	1980–88	1960–70	1970–80	1980–88
UK	2.4	1.3	2.5	3.0	1.6	5.2
US	2.0	0.4	1.2	3.5	3.0	4.0
Japan	8.9	3.8	2.9	8.8	5.3	3.1
Germany	4.4	2.8	1.8	4.1	2.9	2.2
France	4.6	2.8	2.0	5.4	3.2	3.1
Italy	6.3	2.6	2.0	5.4	3.0	3.5
Canada	2.4	1.5	1.4	3.4	3.0	3.6
G7 average	**3.5**	**1.7**	**1.8**	**4.5**	**3.3**	**3.6**

Sources: CSO, OECD, IMF

Table B Relative productivity levels (whole economy 1986)

	GDP per head of population	GDP per person employed	GDP per hour worked
UK	100	100	100
US	150	141	132
Japan	106	94	67
Germany	110	113	105
France	106	119	117
Italy	100	–	–
Canada	140	131	116

Source: OECD
Figures for Italy incomplete because of uncertainties in the size of the hidden economy

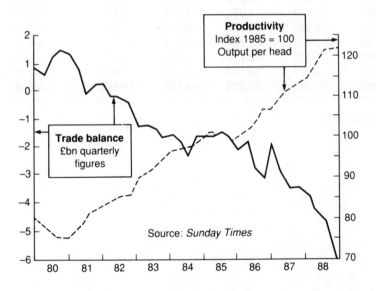

Figure A UK productivity and the visible trade balance (owing to data revisions there may be inconsistencies between Table C and Figure A)

Table C UK trade balances (£ million)

| | Current balance | Visible trade balances | | | Invisible trade balance (Total) |
| | | Total | of which | | |
			Oil	Total manf.	
1970	+ 795	– 34	– 496	+ 2 562	+ 829
1971	+ 1 089	+ 190	– 692	+ 3 015	+ 899
1972	+ 190	– 750	– 666	+ 2 145	+ 939
1973	– 1 018	– 2 586	– 941	+ 1 488	+ 1 568
1974	– 3 316	– 5 350	– 3 357	+ 1 970	+ 2 034
1975	– 1 582	– 3 333	– 3 057	+ 3 737	+ 1 751
1976	– 941	– 3 959	– 3 947	+ 4 917	+ 3 018
1977	– 150	– 2 324	– 2 771	+ 5 886	+ 2 174
1978	+ 964	– 1 593	– 1 984	+ 5 066	+ 2 557
1979	– 496	– 3 398	– 731	+ 2 698	+ 2 902
1980	+ 3 122	+ 1 353	+ 308	+ 5 450	+ 1 769
1981	+ 6 936	+ 3 350	+ 3 105	+ 4 576	+ 3 586
1982	+ 4 685	+ 2 218	+ 4 639	+ 2 297	+ 2 467
1983	+ 3 832	– 1 075	+ 6 972	– 2 448	+ 4 907
1984	+ 2 022	– 4 580	+ 6 932	– 4 054	+ 6 602
1985	+ 3 337	– 2 346	+ 8 101	– 3 151	+ 5 683
1986	– 175	– 8 715	+ 4 065	– 5 710	+ 8 541
1987	– 2 687	– 10 162	+ 4 184	– 7 490	+ 7 475
1988	– 14 271	– 20 336	+ 2 787	– 14 830	+ 6 065

Source: DTI

Chapter Six
Policy implications

No *attempt has ever been made in the* UK *economy to develop a coherent strategy of export-led growth.*

If the process of deindustrialization is to be halted, the trade performance of the manufacturing sector needs to be improved. There are three possible routes:

- improving competitiveness;
- restricting the growth of imports; or
- increasing the rate of growth of exports.

Improving competitiveness
One of the main policy instruments in this context is the exchange rate. An exchange rate depreciation will improve the balance of trade in manufactures provided the demands for exports and imports are sufficiently price-elastic. The specific condition is that the sum of the price elasticities of demand for exports and imports sum to greater than one (the **Marshall–Lerner theorem**). The effect that exchange rate depreciation has on the balance of trade, however, is also dependent on other policies being pursued at the same time, particularly on monetary policy. For example, if a high interest rate policy is being pursued to restrict the demand for credit, this may worsen competitiveness by increasing costs and reducing investment (as well as attracting short-term capital inflows which will tend to offset the depreciation).

The relevance of exchange rate depreciation can also be questioned. Currency depreciation tends to ossify an industrial structure by making countries more competitive in types of goods that may be responsible for balance of payments difficulties in the first place (i.e. the production of 'down-market' goods). Moreover, depreciation would have to be continuous to put a country on a higher *growth* path consistent with balance of payments equilibrium, and it is also highly inflationary: by raising the price of traded goods. As many authors have shown, depreciation cannot be relied upon to improve competitiveness or to rectify balance of payments disequilibrium for a sustained, long time period.

But, in any case, exchange rate adjustment is now virtually precluded by Britain's firm commitment to the European Exchange Rate Mechanism (ERM).

Competitiveness will also be improved if unit labour costs fall relative to other countries. Labour costs per unit of output depend on the money wage rate and the level of labour productivity. If money wage rates can be restrained and labour productivity increases, competitiveness may improve. **Supply side policies** aimed at making the labour and product markets more competitive are regarded by some as being aimed at restraining wage inflation and improving efficiency (see Healey and Levačić, 1992).

Protectionism

Import controls are a possibility but there are many weaknesses and disadvantages of an inward-looking strategy based on import protection.

Firstly, if import controls take the form of tariffs, a once-for-all tariff may reduce the *level* of imports, but it is unlikely to reduce the *rate of growth* of imports permanently, which is what is required if the country is to move to a higher growth path without balance of payments difficulties arising. To reduce the rate of growth of imports permanently would require an ever-increasing tariff level, in the same way that it is recognized that a *continual* depreciation of the currency would achieve the same objective if that were a feasible policy.

Secondly, if price uncompetitiveness is part of the problem, tariffs are a policy of adjusting the **internal price structure** to the **internal cost structure**, while what is required is an adjustment of the internal cost structure to the **external price structure**. The danger is then that once the limits of import substitution have been reached there is no basis for further improvement in the balance of payments. Faster export growth is jeopardized and virtually precluded because an unfavourable internal cost structure has been protected. Many developing countries have paid dearly for this **import substitution strategy** at the expense of promoting exports. If demand is at all important for achieving high levels of output and productivity, and for reaping economies of scale, it is much more sensible to orientate domestic industry to the virtually unlimited world market, as Japan learnt to do a long time ago.

A third disadvantage of tariffs is that, by raising the internal price level, a loss of consumer welfare is incurred. It is true that the revenue gained from tariffs could be used to reduce indirect taxes on goods but there is no guarantee that this would happen.

An alternative form of import control would be **import quotas**. To be effective, however, in reducing permanently the rate of growth of imports, they would have to be comprehensive covering virtually all imports. Otherwise, as demand was expanded there would be some switching from imports with quotas to imports without, and imports would continue to grow. There could also be complex administrative problems in allocating the scarce imports between competing uses.

Whatever form import controls take, however, they are all isolationist and inward-looking. A dynamic growth and development policy cannot be based on protection alone. There must be an **export strategy** as well. The counter-argument to these criticisms has three elements:

- Firstly, import controls work quickly to get an economy back to full employment.
- Secondly, in the movement back to full employment, investment will rise, technological progress will accelerate and average costs of production will fall, producing dynamic benefits which will raise the rate of growth of exports.
- Thirdly, if controls discriminate against countries with a balance of payments surplus this will help to raise the growth of world income and consequently UK exports too.

There is some force in this counter-argument, but it requires a very much greater act of faith to believe in dynamic benefits stemming from import controls than in the benefits that could accrue from an investment and taxation policy deliberately orientated to raising the rate of growth of exports. The dynamic benefits from import controls are supposed to arise as firms move along downward-sloping average-cost curves towards full capacity utilization. There can be little doubt that cost curves are downward-sloping at less than full employment, but what happens under this strategy when full employment is reached and there is no more scope for import substitution? The dynamism produced by import restrictions ceases. By contrast, an investment policy to encourage exports, which also relieved the balance of payments constraint on demand, would also move firms along the same downward-sloping cost curves; but at the same time, by inducing structural change, the policy could put exports and hence the economy on a permanently higher growth path. Import controls and import substitution may be a quicker route to full employment than an industrial strategy to raise exports, but they are inferior as a growth strategy if export growth remains unchanged.

The policy of import restrictions will also no doubt help to raise the growth of world income provided the composition of imports is altered against those countries with balance of payments surpluses. However, if the world income elasticity of demand for UK exports is lower than for other countries (which it is), a rise in the growth of world income will *worsen* the *relative* performance of the UK economy. In other words, a policy of import restrictions does nothing to raise the propensity of other countries to buy UK goods and thus would simply consolidate the UK's position at the bottom of the growth league table as far as exports are concerned. By contrast, if an investment strategy, working through the tax system, could induce structural change in favour of activities producing goods with a high income elasticity of demand in world markets, the growth of world income would be raised in the same way as under import controls (by relieving the economy of the balance of payments constraint on demand), and at the same time the growth rate of UK exports would be higher and hence the overall growth of output.

Those who advocate import controls are understandably preoccupied with the short-run, but there is also a need to stand back to consider the longer-run issue of the UK economy's chronically slow underlying average growth rate over the post-war years compared with other developed countries. All the evidence suggests that a necessary condition for a faster long-run rate of growth of output and living standards is a faster rate of growth of exports, which import controls do nothing to foster directly. If intercountry differences in export and import propensities are examined, it is not so much the overall UK import propensity which looks so alarming but the abysmally slow growth of exports compared with other countries. This, in turn, seems to have very little to do with relative price differences, but with a very low income elasticity of demand for UK goods in world markets owing mainly to the supply characteristics of the goods such as their design, reliability, delivery, marketing, servicing and quality in the widest sense.

Regardless of 'quality', we also know that some goods have an intrinsically lower income elasticity of demand because they are 'inferior' goods (goods produced to cater for low-income markets as opposed to high-income markets). There is no hope of improving this fundamental weakness by import controls (or by currency depreciation for that matter).

An import control strategy would also, of course, run directly counter to the **Treaty of Rome** and jeopardize Britain's membership of the EC. A more promising and acceptable approach to Britain's foreign trade weakness would be to promote exports.

Export-led growth

No attempt has ever been made in the UK economy to develop a coherent strategy of export-led growth. The primary task of economic policy in the United Kingdom must be to develop a strategy of export-led growth based on a judicious mix of taxes and subsidies to alter the allocation of investment resources and the composition of output in favour of exports. UK export performance is a function of the *types* of goods produced and the *division* of output between domestic and foreign markets. **Tax incentives** could be used both to alter the structure of production and to raise export performance within the structure. The **structural change** required is to induce an allocation of resources in favour of technologically progressive industries producing goods with a high income elasticity of demand in world markets. The policy could be integrated with an **industrial strategy** and linked to a system of **investment grants** and allowances. Investment incentives could be discriminatory according to various growth criteria.

A complementary strategy – or a second-best to the first if the idea of discrimination offends the British sense of fair-play – would be to relate

investment grants and allowances to the proportion of output exported. This would tend to bias both the structure of output and the composition of output towards exports if manufacturers are at all responsive to differential rates of return. In addition, it would be possible simply to make exporting more profitable by remitting corporation tax on export earnings.

A number of other things could be done: exporting firms might be offered cheaper credit for investment; an attempt could be made to raise the status of marketing in firms; encouragement could be given to foreign-language training, and to finding room for engineers in the board-rooms of firms.

Such an export-led growth strategy, however, violates international trading agreements – in particular, Article 92 of the Treaty of Rome which lays down that state aids which distort competition are incompatible with the Common Market. It does specify, however, two forms of permissible 'regional' aid: (1) aid intended to promote economic development in regions where there is a low standard of living or serious under-employment, and (2) aid intended to facilitate the development of *particular activities* or economic regions, provided that it does not affect trading conditions adversely. In one sense, any subsidy or tax concession to any activity distorts 'free competition'. On the other hand, free competition itself may affect trading conditions adversely if it means that a country languishes economically and under-utilizes its resources. In these circumstances, support for activities to achieve a fuller utilization of resources could enhance the volume of trade for all. It is in this spirit that support for export activities within regional groupings should be assessed.

It is interesting to note that Article XII of the **GATT agreement**, originally signed in 1948, permits control over imports for the same balance of payments reasons, and countries adversely affected are not permitted to impose counter-measures. Given the UK's long-term economic dilemma and the massive full-employment deficit on the current account of the balance of payments, one might hope that there would be a good deal of international sympathy for the kind of strategy here outlined, whether Britain remains a member of GATT and the EC or not. At least the water could be tested, as other EC countries have done from time to time with respect to both import restrictions and export promotion. Just how far a weak country could go would be interesting to see.

With the creation of a single European market in 1992, some mechanism is required to permit countries to deal with structural balance of payments problems and the associated poor economic performance.

Current EC policy in this field involves the payment of development grants (from the European Regional Development Fund) to finance investment in depressed regions. While the Fund has mainly been used to finance investment in infrastructure projects, it is also seen as a means of regenerating areas with high unemployment. This mechanism is unlikely to be sufficient to deal with the structural imbalances that currently exist and which are likely to intensify after 1992.

KEY WORDS

Competitiveness	Import quotas
Marshall–Lerner theorem	Export strategy
Supply side policies	Treaty of Rome
Protectionism	Export-led growth
Import controls	Tax incentives
Internal price structure	Structural change
Internal cost structure	Industrial strategy
External price structure	Investment grants
Import substitution strategy	GATT agreement

Reading list

Healey, N. and Levačić, R., *Supply Side Economics,* 2nd edn, Heinemann Educational, 1992.

Mathews, K., 'Britain's economic renaissance', *Economics,* autumn 1989.

Robinson, B., 'How fast dare we grow?', *Economic Review*, vol. 5, March 1988.

Thirlwall, A.P. and Gibson, H.D., *Balance of Payments Theory and the UK Experience*, 4th edn, Macmillan, 1992.

Essay topics

1. 'UK governments in the 1980s were primarily concerned about increasing incentives, generating greater competition and eliminating market imperfections.' Outline the various policies which were implemented to achieve these objectives. On what criteria could the effectiveness of these policies be evaluated? (University of London School Examinations Board, 1991)

2. What are supply side policies? Can such policies lead to an improvement in a country's economic performance? (Associated Examining Board, 1991)
3. What do you understand by the phrase 'conflict of policy objectives'? To what extent is the UK's ability to pursue domestic economic policies limited by balance of payments constraints? (University of London School Examinations Board, 1991)

Data Response Question 6

Whither the trade deficit?

This task is based on a question set by the University of London School Examinations Board in 1992. Read the extract below, which is adapted from *The Times* of 15 February 1988, and answer the following questions.

1. What is meant by 'UK competitiveness'?
2. Analyse the reasoning behind the statement that 'The prospect of a major balance of payments crisis remains the single most important danger for the UK economy in 1988'.
3. How may the 'strength of domestic demand in the UK relative to its trading partners' cause balance of payments problems?
4. Examine one short-term and one long-term measure likely to reduce the UK's balance of payments deficit.

The prospect of a major balance of payments crisis remains the single most important danger for the UK economy in 1988. The re-emergence of the external constraint will be increasingly important in framing monetary policy through the year.

The manufacturing deficit looks set to worsen further due to two critical factors. The first is the UK's competitiveness. The restrained growth in unit labour costs in 1987 owed a great deal to rapid productivity growth on the back of sharply expanding production. In 1988 pro-duction will grow less rapidly, productivity gains will be slow, and unit labour costs could expand sharply.

Meanwhile, the exchange rate will not be allowed to come to the rescue on present policies.

The second factor is the strength of domestic demand in the UK relative to its main trading partners. The OECD forecast real domestic demand growth of $3\frac{3}{4}\%$ in the UK, $2\frac{1}{2}\%$ in the EEC as a whole and only 1% in the US. Under these circumstances the trend for the UK trade deficit has only one direction to go.

Chapter Seven

The future

'The improvement of UK performance depends both on an improved allocation of resources for invention and innovation and a much more efficient exploitation of the potential advantages to be derived from technical innovation.' C. Freeman.

In Chapter 5 the events and consequences of the recession of 1979–82 were examined. The period 1989–91 witnessed another severe recession, following a monetary-induced boom in the preceding three years. Stop–go, go–stop has characterized economic policy making for the last 40 years, but since 1979 the economic cycles have been the more pronounced as a result of what can only be described as serious economic mismanagement. Mrs Thatcher's economic philosophy was one of fiscal rectitude, balanced budgets, an abrogation of the commitment to full employment ('there is no alternative', and 'governments cannot spend their way out of unemployment', she said). The whole approach of macroeconomic policy was essentially non-interventionist, relying on the private sector to reach an equilibrium through market forces, with the government pursuing supply-side policies to reduce the fiscal and bureaucratic burdens on business, to liberalize product markets and to remove 'imperfections' in the labour market. The overriding macro-objective was to squeeze inflation out of the system, apparently at any cost. This framework broadly prevailed until 1986/87 when a combination of tax cuts and lax monetary policy, under the Chancellorship of Mr Lawson, sparked off a consumer-led boom, causing inflation to accelerate and the balance of payments to go into deep deficit to the tune of nearly £20 billion in 1989. The government's response was to tighten monetary policy again by raising interest rates to over 15 per cent, which caused GDP to contract by 2 per cent in 1990, and unemployment to soar. Interest rates were brought down close to 10 per cent in 1991, but the economy remained sluggish with unemployment at 2.4 million and rising. Mindful, no doubt, of the necessity of a General Election in 1992, the Autumn Statement of Public Expenditure in 1991 *planned* for a budget deficit of approximately £20 billion. The newspapers heralded the rehabilitation of fiscal policy and the return of Keynesian demand management, which must have caused Mrs Thatcher much anguish (having relinquished the premiership to John Major in 1990). Whether this fiscal expansion and further promised tax cuts will usher in another mini-boom remains to be seen.

The **long term**, however, remains bleak. Investment and output in the manufacturing sector continues to languish, the growth of labour productivity (after a spurt in the early 1980s) has reverted to its former trend, and the peak of every cycle seems to be associated with successively higher levels of unemployment and a worsening balance of payments position. The important questions relate to whether economic growth can be sustained sufficiently long on current policies to beat the scourge of unemployment, and bring it down at least to one million. With unemployment in 1991 at 2.4 million and forecast to continue rising despite the official end of recession (because employment growth lags behind output growth), it is unlikely that even the fiscal stimulus of 1991/92 will make much impact. The long-term prospect is bleak because current economic policies do nothing to address the **structural problems** that contribute to the poor performance of the UK economy in the medium and long term. In particular, the balance of payments equilibrium growth rate will need to be raised.

We are not optimistic about the future for two major reasons. Firstly, North Sea oil revenues are declining and will continue to decline. Nothing can be done about the deflation of this cushion, which until recently helped to fill the growing gap between manufactured imports and exports, unless a dramatic rise in oil prices leads to further exploration and oil discoveries. Furthermore, it is unlikely that exports of services will grow sufficiently to fill the gap left by oil, let alone to offset the growing balance of trade deficit in manufactures. The second worry concerns the implications for British manufacturing industry of the **single European market.**

1992 and All That

The onset of the single European market in 1992, in which all barriers to trade in goods and factors of production disappear, is a major step along the way to complete European integration. If past experience is anything to go by, however, the prospects for British industry look bleak.

Britain remained outside the EC until 1973. It then became a member on the pretext that access to a larger market would enable industry

EC integration 'threatens industry'

European industry is heading for a drastic and painful restructuring which will lead to the disappearance of many companies and could create higher unemployment in the next few years, several business leaders warned yesterday.

They expected these threatened upheavals to fuel pressures in the European Community for at least temporary trade protection against third countries, particularly Japan. EC governments could find such demands increasingly hard to resist.

The forecasts, made at a Financial Times conference in London, suggest that the recent euphoria generated by the EC's single market plan is starting to dissipate as companies face fiercer competition.

Sir John Harvey-Jones, chairman of Parallax Enterprises and former chairman of ICI, said that in the next 10 years more than half of Europe's factories would be closed and half its companies would disappear or be absorbed by mergers.

He was optimistic that a more integrated European market would be achieved, but said: "We are going to see on our road to Nirvana degrees of pain which, if governments react, as they normally do, they will seek to relieve through protection."

Mr Percy Barnevik, chairman of ABB, the recently merged Swedish-Swiss heavy engineering group, said it would not be easy for the EC simultaneously to restructure overcrowded sectors and to open its market to competition from Japan and South Korea.

There were 13 locomotive builders in Europe, compared with two in the US and three to four in Japan. A reduction was necessary to increase efficiency but would lead to higher unemployment, which would take time to absorb.

"These are the hard realities behind the nice words higher productivity and more competitive," he said. Political sensitivities would make restructuring even harder in Europe's poorer regions.

Mr Barnevik said that only a third of European companies would see themselves as winners from increased cross-border trade in a single market, while two-thirds would see themselves as losers.

Mr Robert Eaton, president of General Motors Europe, said severe cuts could be forced on European car makers if national restrictions on Japanese car imports were lifted.

The Japanese share of the European new car market could rise to as much as 30 per cent from the current 11 per cent, threatening about 10 big assembly plants and as many as 300 000 jobs in Europe. "It is not difficult to assume that it could be mainly the Japanese who will be the major beneficiaries of a unified single market," said Mr Eaton.

Though trade protection would only lull European industry into false complacency, it could become hard to resist, particularly if countries such as Japan and South Korea continued to promote their industries at the expense of their trading partners.

Source: *Financial Times*,
23 November 1988

to reap economies of large-scale production and therefore enhance its competitiveness. More competition and less protection was to blow the cobwebs off British industry and enable it to compete more effectively in international markets. A government White Paper in 1970 entitled *Britain and the European Communities: An Economic Assessment* (Cmnd 4289) argued that there would be:

> '... dynamic effects resulting from membership of a much larger and faster growing market. This would open up to our industrial producers substantial opportunities for increasing export sales, while at the same time exposing them more fully to the competition of European industries. No way has been found of quantifying these dynamic benefits, but if British industry responded vigorously to the stimuli, they would be considerable and highly advantageous. The acceleration of the rate of growth of industrial exports could then outpace any increase in the rate of growth of imports, with corresponding benefits to the balance of payments. Moreover, with such a response, the growth of industrial productivity would be accelerated as a result of increased competition and the advantages derived from specialization and larger scale production. This faster rate of growth would, in turn, accelerate the rate of growth of national production and real income.'

A further White Paper in 1971, *The United Kingdom and the European Communities* (Cmnd 4715), promised much of the same. The miserable economic performance of the British economy was compared with the vastly superior performance of the EC, with the optimism expressed that:

> 'Her Majesty's Government is convinced that our economy [will be] stronger and our industries and peoples more prosperous if we join the European Communities than if we remain outside them. ...Improvements in efficiency and competitive power should enable the UK to meet the balance of payments costs of entry over the next decade as they gradually build up. ... [The] advantages will far outweigh the costs, provided we seize the opportunities of the far wider home market now open to us.'

The much-heralded beneficial winds of change turned into a gale of destruction for much of manufacturing industry, as might have been predicted from both economic theory and experience that when weak countries join **free-trade** areas or customs unions, the strong countries benefit at their expense. There is nothing in the doctrine of free trade that says that the **gains from trade** will be equally distributed among partners. Indeed, some countries may lose *absolutely* if the gains from specialization that free trade permits are offset by the unemployment of resources which comes about if import growth exceeds export growth, and the growth of output internally has to be constrained because of balance of payments difficulties. The doctrine of free trade ignores the balance of payments implications, implicitly assuming that the balance of payments looks after itself and that full employment is maintained.

There is precious little evidence that Britain joining the EC has raised the underlying growth rate of the British economy consistent with balance of payments equilibrium. On the contrary, there is evidence that the budgetary costs of entry, the extent of import penetration from Europe, and a growing trade imbalance in manufactures, particularly with Germany, have tightened the balance of payments constraint on Britain's growth rate.

The balance tilted against UK recovery

BILL MARTIN (UBS Phillips & Drew)

Britain's economic debate has become hopelessly politicised and short-term. Every new fragile statistic and volatile survey is pounced upon in a frenetic search for those green shoots of recovery which the Chancellor fervently hopes will blossom forth this side of the General Election. So for one blessed moment, forget the political economy and consider something which really matters.

This year [1991], at the bottom of deep recession, the UK is running an unprecedented current account deficit. It is not, of course, the biggest deficit ever recorded. In 1989, the then Chancellor, Nigel Lawson, presided over a £20bn deficit, 4 per cent of the nation's gross domestic product. As a proportion of GDP, there was a similar-sized deficit under a Labour Chancellor in 1974, though he could rightly blame Britain's swollen oil trade deficit, enlarged by the global price rise. This year, on Treasury figures, Norman Lamont will have succeeded in reducing the current account deficit to a mere £6.5bn, a figure flattered by £2bn of Gulf war contributions and unusually low net contributions by the UK to the European Community.

The 1991 deficit – excluding the volatile oil balance – is nevertheless unprecedented in Britain's post-war history. In previous recession years, the economy always generated current account surpluses, ex-oil, averaging 1.75 per cent of GDP. Excluding oil and those flattering contributions, the comparable 1991 figure is of the same magnitude, but with a reverse sign. That amounts to a trade deficiency equal to 3.5 per cent of GDP. The current account is £20bn out of true.

What has gone wrong? After all, British industry did improve its performance fundamentally during the Eighties. Thanks to the decline in union power and improvements in managerial efficiency, the level of productivity in UK manufacturing was brought towards that achieved in Continental Europe. This catch-up should continue, aided by foreign implants.

The UK has efficient companies. Its problem is that it does not have enough of them in the right places. There has emerged over the past decade a staggering imbalance between the capacity of the economy's internationally trading sector, principally manufacturing, and the level of domestic spending. It is this gap which lies behind the fundamental deterioration in the UK's current account performance through the Eighties.

Seventies and a roller-coaster through the Eighties. This year, capacity is likely to fall by 3 per cent, as a result of the collapse in investment, now thankfully nearing an end, and the high rates of plant scrapping.

Since 1979, manufacturing capacity has therefore hardly increased – up a mere 2 per cent. By contrast, the volume of domestic demand – consumer spending and investment – has grown impressively, up nearly 30 per cent. This fearful asymmetry has produced an economy in serious structural imbalance.

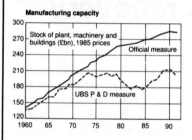

Manufacturing capacity

Stock of plant, machinery and buildings (£bn), 1985 prices

Official measure

UBS P & D measure

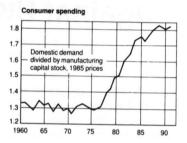

Consumer spending

Domestic demand divided by manufacturing capital stock, 1985 prices

It is not too difficult to measure the size of manufacturing capacity in terms of plant and machinery, as long as one ignores the official figures. The official estimates of the capital stock are produced by an elegant computer algorithm which is wonderfully divorced from the real world. The preferable procedure is to derive figures from estimates of output combined with manufacturers' own assessment of plant capacity utilisation rates in the CBI survey.

The survey-based estimates shown in the first chart tell a tale which any industrialist would recognise. A strong expansion of manufacturing capacity in the Sixties gave way to stagnation in the

The result of all this is that Britain's growth rate over the medium term will be balance-of-payments constrained. Eminent commentators who dismiss the current account deficit as an irrelevance are themselves living in dreamland. It is wholly implausible that autonomous capital inflows would accommodate a continued and major escalation in Britain's deficit from today's levels. Indeed, according to a recent scholarly study from the Bank for International Settlements, the changing nature of global capital markets during the Nineties may make it more, not less difficult to finance current account imbalances.

Source: *Independent on Sunday*, 17 November 1991

The year 1992 was set for the complete liberalization of trade and the removal of all restrictions on the movement of capital and labour within the EC. The European Commission in Brussels is predicting substantial benefits, including a 4.5 per cent rise in GDP in the Community as a whole, a 6 per cent reduction in prices, and employment gains of 1.8 million; but it says nothing about the *distribution* of gains between member countries.

These further moves towards liberalization can only, in our view, strengthen the **centrifugal forces** already apparent within the Community by which the rich regions and countries get richer and the poor, poorer. 1992 does not augur well, therefore, for British industry, or for the British economy which is still chronically weak.

There can be no guarantee that the **mobility of factors of production**, such as labour and capital, between countries will equalize the rewards to factors of production, as orthodox (neoclassical) theory predicts, and that therefore per capita income levels will be equalized between countries. Orthodox theory says that factors of production migrate in

response to differences in economic opportunity – and this is true – but the predictions of the theory seem to conflict with the facts. As labour migrates from a depressed to a more prosperous region or country, the supply of labour and unemployment is supposed to fall in the depressed region (with the demand for labour unchanged), so that wages rise, while in the more prosperous regions the increased supply of labour (with demand unchanged) is supposed to depress wages. Capital is supposed to 'migrate' the other way from prosperous regions where the wage rate is higher (and the rate of profit lower) to depressed regions where the wage rate is lower (and the rate of profit higher).

That is the neoclassical story, but it is a very static story which ignores the dynamic interactions between the supply and demand for factors of production as migration takes place. For example, as labour migration takes place it brings with it its own demands – in the form of demand for local goods, the provision of local services, housing and so on – so that the demand for labour increases with the supply of labour in the prosperous region, while in the depressed region from which the migrants come, the demand is depressed. The equilibration of wages may not take place.

Likewise, as far as capital is concerned, the location of regional investment is not simply a function of relative wage rates, but also a function of productivity and the expected strength of demand. Therefore new investment is just as likely to flow to prosperous regions to which people are migrating as to depressed regions where the wages may be lower. Investment and employment growth tend to be complementary in the productive process.

All this is to say that initial differences in the level of development between regions and/or countries do not necessarily set up forces which eliminate those differences. On the contrary, forces are set up which may perpetuate and even widen these differences. The operation of these forces has been called by the Swedish economist, Gunnar Myrdal, the 'process of **circular and cumulative causation**'. These forces are factor mobility and free trade which lead to '**virtuous circles** of growth' in strong regions and countries and '**vicious circles** of poverty' in weak regions and countries. If the theory of circular and cumulative causation is correct, liberalization in 1992 will further widen regional/country disparities in levels of prosperity in Europe.

It must not be forgotten, too, that Britain is not only economically weak and relatively poor compared with many of its partners; it also lies on the *geographic periphery of Europe*. It is not in the 'centre' of the market for goods and services, but it is the 'centre' of a market that always exerts a strong gravitational pull. It is not an economic accident that the relatively depressed regions of the UK are on the geographic periphery of the UK or that many of the depressed regions of the EC lie on the geographic periphery of Europe.

There is reason to be worried for the future, not only as a result of the effects of the operation of free-market forces pulling investment and skilled labour from Britain to the centre of Europe, but also because the Articles of Agreement of the EC make it increasingly difficult for countries to pursue an independent economic policy, at least as far as the functioning of the real economy is concerned.

It cannot offer incentives to industrial development because that means unfair competition; it cannot discriminate in favour of particular activities because that distorts competition; and it cannot restrict trade. Furthermore, if the idea of complete **monetary union** was adopted, with a European Central Bank and a **single currency**, countries would lose control over exchange rate policy and monetary policy as well. Britain in Europe would become like Scotland, or Wales, or any other region within the UK, or like the states within the USA; that is, completely at the mercy of market forces as far as economic performance is concerned, devoid of any instruments of economic policy, and with depressed regions dependent on the largesse of a central administration. This must be the worry for British industry, and therefore the British economy, in the 1990s.

KEY WORDS

Long term	Mobility of factors of
Structural problems	production
Single European market	Circular and cumulative
Free trade	causation
Gains from trade	Virtuous and vicious circles
Centrifugal forces	Monetary Union
	Single Currency

Reading list

Aldcroft, D., 'Policy responses to industrial decline', *Economic Review*, vol. 5, May 1988.

Ball, Sir J., 'The UK economy: miracle or mirage?', *National Westminster Bank Quarterly Review*, Feb. 1989.

Healey, N. and Levačić, R., *Supply Side Economics,* 2nd edn, Heinemann Educational, 1992.

Smith, D., *Mrs Thatcher's Economics: Her Legacy*, 2nd edn, Heinemann Educational, 1992.

Essay topics

1. Analysè the factors which have led to the deindustrialization of the UK economy since 1970. Discuss whether the completion of a Single European Market will accelerate deindustrialization. (Combined boards of Oxford & Cambridge/Cambridge Local, AS-level, 1991)
2. What do you understand by 'full employment'? Critically discuss the view that full employment is no longer an achievable objective of economic policy in the UK. (Associated Examining Board, 1988)
3. What are the causes of unemployment in the UK? Explain and evaluate the measures you would advocate to reduce the level of unemployment in the UK. (University of Cambridge Local Examinations Syndicate, 1991)

Data Response Question 7

Manufacturing employment in OECD countries

This task is based on a question set by Oxford & Cambridge Schools Examination Board/University of Cambridge Local Examinations Syndicate (at AS-level) in 1991. Refer back to Table 4 on page 15 of this book and answer the following questions.

1. Compare the extent of deindustrialization in the UK with other OECD countries.
2. Comment upon the likely economic implications of deindustrialization in the UK and other OECD countries.

Postscript

*'Economic historians will, I believe, look back with incredulity at this
episode in British history.'*   A.P. Thirlwall

═══

The article you are about to read appeared in *The Age* (an Australian
daily newspaper) on 29 September 1988. It is based on a talk given by
one of us (A.P.T.) during a visit to the University of Melbourne's
Economics Department. The article was published under the title 'The
myth of the Thatcher miracle'.

*   *   *

Since arriving in Australia two weeks ago for a brief academic visit, I
keep hearing references to an alleged British economic miracle. There
appears to be a widespread belief that nine years of Conservative government under Mrs Thatcher has resulted in a radical transformation
of the British economy and a marked improvement in its potential for
faster growth on a sustainable basis.

I am afraid to say that this is a myth. There has been no 'supply-side'
revolution; the inertia and conservatism of British business, finance and
other institutions remains, and the British economy is no closer to
finding a solution to the simultaneous achievement of faster growth,
full employment, stable prices and balance of payments equilibrium
than it was before the 'Thatcher experiment' of monetarism,
privatisation, trade union reform, tax reductions and rolling back the
frontiers of the state.

What is being witnessed in Britain at the moment is a short-run
unsustainable boom fuelled by consumption and this follows the
deepest recession ever experienced in the British economy, which was
deliberately engineered between 1979 and 1981 to curb the power of
trade unions and to squeeze inflation out of the system. To argue my
case, it is necessary to go back into history.

In the three decades following World War II, the British economy
experienced the lowest rate of economic growth of any major
industrialized country – averaging 2.5 per cent a year. Britain slipped
from being one of the richest countries in the world to 19th in the per
capita income stakes. The investment record was good by historical
standards, but poor by international comparisons. The industrial

relations record was generally appalling and the management of British industry weak.

The economy was perpetually plagued by balance of payments problems. The growth of export volume was the slowest of all OECD countries, while the country's appetite for foreign manufactured goods appeared insatiable. The effect of these adverse factors combined to produce deindustrialization on a vast scale, with a loss of jobs in manufacturing industry of over two million between 1966 and 1979.

THE fatal policy mistake was to favor current consumption at the expense of investment and the foreign trade sector. In 1963, aware that living standards were falling relative to Europe, there was a dash for growth which precipitated the worst balance of payments crisis in history (till then) and contributed to the election of a Labor government in 1964.

The Labor administration put its faith in indicative planning and published a National Plan, setting a target growth rate of 4.5 per cent per annum. The need to deflate to tackle the balance of payments, however, made a nonsense of the plan, and it was soon abandoned.

The Pavlovian response was to look to the Common Market (EEC) for salvation. The predictions of economic theory that within customs unions the weak get weaker and the strong get stronger were ignored. Britain joined the EEC in 1973 and some of the worst fears of the critics of entry have materialised.

The trade deficit in manufactured goods, particularly with Germany, has risen by alarming proportions, and in many spheres of economic life it is now no longer possible to pursue an independent economic policy.

In the late 1960s the spectre of inflation began to rear its ugly head. This was fuelled by sterling devaluation in 1967 and aggressive trade union behavior, and later exacerbated by the commodity price boom of the early 1970s.

Neither the Conservatives between 1970 and 1974 nor the Labor Party between 1974 and 1979 were able to slay the dragon. The trade unions will still not admit that wage inflation is a major source of price inflation (independent of prior increases in the money supply), and the Labor Party – a prisoner of the trade unions – will still not publicly advocate incomes policy.

It was largely the irresponsible behavior of the trade unions, and the serious inflation of the late 1970s, that brought Mrs Thatcher to power in 1979.

The 'Iron Lady' came into office determined to reduce the role of the state in economic affairs; to end all forms of corporatism, and to weaken the power of the trade unions on the assumption that excessive government intervention and the power of the unions have been the major sources of Britain's long-term economic malaise.

So, the vital question remains, has nine years of Thatcherism made any difference?

The first three years of Mrs Thatcher's reign turned out to be an economic nightmare. Notwithstanding the cushion of North Sea oil, the Government managed to engineer the biggest recession in recorded history – worse than the great depression of the 1930s. Between 1979 and 1981 total output fell by three per cent and unemployment rose from one million to 2.5 million.

Monetary and fiscal policy was exceedingly tight, and the effective exchange rate rose by over 20 per cent which also contributed to the recession.

As justification, it is sometimes argued that a cathartic exercise was necessary on the assumption that leaner means fitter, and out of the ashes some phoenix would rise. For much of British industry, however, leaner meant not fitter but strangulation and even death. Manufacturing output has only now reached again its 1979 level.

This economic masochism coincided with annual flows of tax revenue and foreign exchange from North Sea oil of close to £10 billion, for which the British economy has nothing to show. The revenue was frittered away in dole payments and expenditure on foreign imports. Economic historians will, I believe, look back with incredulity at this episode in British economic history.

Since 1982 there has been a general recovery of output and employment, and currently the economy is growing at close to four per cent a year. The Government and press proclaim an economic miracle, justifying the earlier sacrifice. I view the situation as more like someone having deliberately thrown themselves off a cliff and then congratulating themselves at having nearly climbed back to the top.

For the fact is that if the Thatcher years are taken as a whole, the average annual growth of GDP is only two per cent, investment is only recently back to its 1979 level; unemployment is still more than double what it was in 1979, and the country is heading for a huge balance of payments crisis like days of old.

The major achievement has been the control of inflation through the crude weapon of unemployment. The reduction of inflation had nothing directly to do with the pursuit of monetarist policies, since the chosen nominal money supply target (M3) proved to be uncontrollable. But even with unemployment at over two million, the inflation rate is starting to rise again.

Likewise, there have been some welcome trade union reforms, and the number of strikes has fallen dramatically, but this is also largely a function of the high levels of unemployment.

Table 16 Macroeconomic indicators by political regimes

	Growth of GDP(%)	Inflation rate(%)	Unemployment percentage
		(annual averages)	
Conservatives 1951–1964	3.2	3.5	1.7
Labour 1964–1970	2.4	5.2	2.0
Conservatives 1970–1974	2.4	11.7	3.1
Labour 1974–1979	1.8	21.2	4.7
Conservatives 1979–1988	2.0	8.4	9.5

State industries and public corporations have been sold off at a handsome profit to speculators, but the management of the enterprises remains exactly the same.

Tax rates have been reduced, particularly for the better off, but no economic research can find any evidence that this makes any significant difference to work effort. The price has been a deterioration in many of the public services. The division between rich and poor has widened, as has the geographic divide between the depressed north of the country and the more affluent south.

BRITAIN'S Achilles heel is still its balance of payments, but the Government shows no sign of appreciating either the nature or magnitude of the problem. The forecast deficit on current account for 1988 is now £15 billion, four times greater than the deficit forecast in the April budget.

The British economic miracle is a mirage, but brilliantly propagandised by the media.

Your chance to provide a solution

This question is designed to allow you the opportunity to put your own interpretation on the facts as they have been presented in this book.

When you have read the foregoing Postscript, attempt the following projects. Remember that you can agree or disagree with the author's *interpretation* of the facts.

1. Draft a critical letter to the Editor of *The Age*, either generally supporting the published article or offering alternative thoughts.
2. Prepare a short newspaper article, intended for a general readership, entitled 'Economic miracle of the 1980s: fact or fiction?'

Index